By Joel Chandler Harris.

NIGHTS WITH UNCLE REMUS. Myths and Legends of the Old Plantation. Illustrated. 12mo, $1.50; paper, 50 cents.

MINGO, and other Sketches in Black and White. 16mo, $1.25; paper, 50 cents.

BALAAM AND HIS MASTER, and other Sketches and Stories. 16mo, $1.25.

HOUGHTON, MIFFLIN & CO.
BOSTON AND NEW YORK.

BALAAM AND HIS MASTER

AND OTHER SKETCHES AND STORIES

BY

JOEL CHANDLER HARRIS

AUTHOR OF "UNCLE REMUS, HIS SONGS AND HIS SAYINGS," "FREE JOE," "DADDY JAKE, THE RUNAWAY," ETC.

BOSTON AND NEW YORK
HOUGHTON, MIFFLIN AND COMPANY
The Riverside Press, Cambridge
1891

Copyright, 1891,
By JOEL CHANDLER HARRIS.

All rights reserved.

The Riverside Press, Cambridge, Mass., U. S. A.
Electrotyped and Printed by H. O. Houghton & Co.

CONTENTS.

	PAGE
BALAAM AND HIS MASTER	7
A CONSCRIPT'S CHRISTMAS	45
ANANIAS	112
WHERE'S DUNCAN?	149
MOM BI	170
THE OLD BASCOM PLACE	192

BALAAM AND HIS MASTER.

WHAT fantastic tricks are played by fate or circumstance! Here is a horrible war that shall redeem a nation, that shall restore civilization, that shall establish Christianity. Here is a university of slavery that shall lead the savage to citizenship. Here is a conflagration that shall rebuild a city. Here is the stroke of a pen that shall change the destinies of many peoples. Here is the bundle of fagots that shall light the fires of liberty. As in great things, so in small. Tragedy drags comedy across the stage, and hard upon the heels of the hero tread the heavy villain and the painted clown.

What a preface to write before the name of Billville!

Years ago, when one of the ex-Virginian pioneers who had settled in Wilkes County, in the State of Georgia, concluded to try his fortune farther west, he found himself, after a tedious journey of a dozen days, in the midst of a little settlement in middle Georgia. His wagons and his negroes were at once surrounded by a crowd of curious but good-humored men and a swarm of tow-headed children.

"What is your name?" he asked one of the group.

"Bill Jones."

"And yours?" turning to another.

"Bill Satterlee."

The group was not a large one, but in addition to Jones and Satterlee, as the newcomer was informed, Bill Ware, Bill Cosby, Bill Pinkerton, Bill Pearson, Bill Johnson, Bill Thurman, Bill Jessup, and Bill Prior were there present, and ready to answer to their names. In short, fate or circumstance had played one of its fantastic pranks in this isolated community, and every male member of the settlement, with the exception of Laban Davis, who was small and puny-looking, bore the name of Bill.

"Well," said the pioneer, who was not without humor, "I'll pitch my tent in Billville. My name is Bill Cozart."

This is how Billville got its name — a name that has clung to it through thick and thin. A justifiable but futile attempt was

made during the war to change the name of
the town to Panola, but it is still called
Billville, much to the disappointment of
those citizens who have drawn both pride
and prosperity in the lottery of life.

It was a fortunate day for Billville when
Mr. William Cozart, almost by accident,
planted his family tree in the soil of the settlement. He was a man of affairs, and at
once became the leading citizen of the place.
His energy and public spirit, which had
room for development here, appeared to be
contagious. He bought hundreds of acres
of land, in the old Virginia fashion, and
made for himself a home as comfortable as
it was costly. His busy and unselfish life
was an example for his neighbors to follow,
and when he died the memory of it was a
precious heritage to his children.

Meanwhile Billville, stirred into action
by his influence, grew into a thrifty village,
and then into a flourishing town; but
through all the changes the Cozarts remained the leading family, socially, politically, and financially. But one day in the
thirties Berrien Cozart was born, and the
wind that blew aside the rich lace of his
cradle must have been an ill one, for the

child grew up to be a thorn in the side of those who loved him best. His one redeeming quality was his extraordinary beauty. This has, no doubt, been exaggerated; but there are still living in Billville many men and women who knew him, and they will tell you to-day that Berrien Cozart was the handsomest man they have ever seen — and some of them have visited every court in Europe. So far as they are concerned, the old saying, "Handsome is that handsome does," has lost its force. They will tell you that Berrien Cozart was the handsomest man in the world and — probably the worst.

He was willful and wrongheaded from the first. He never, even as a child, acknowledged any authority but his own sweet will. He could simulate obedience whenever it suited his purpose, but only one person in the world had any real influence over him — a negro named Balaam. The day Berrien Cozart was born, his proud and happy father called to a likely negro lad who was playing about in the yard — the day was Sunday — and said: —

"How old are you?"

"I dunno 'zackly, marster, but ole Aunt Emmeline she know."

"Do you do any work?"

"Yes, suh; I totes water, an' I drives de cows ter de pastur', an' I keeps off de calfs, an' I runs de chickens out 'n de gyardin."

The sprightly and intelligent appearance of the lad evidently made a favorable impression on the master, for he beckoned to him and said: —

"Come in here; I want to show you something."

The negro dropped his hat on the ground and followed Mr. Cozart, who led the way to the darkened room where Berrien, the baby, was having his first experience with existence. He lay on the nurse's lap, with blinking eyes and red and wrinkled face, trying to find his mouth with his fists. The nurse, black as she was, was officious, and when she saw the negro boy she exclaimed: —

"Balaam, w'at you doin' in yere? Take yo'se'f right out! Dis ain't no place fer you."

"Marster says so," said Balaam, sententiously.

"Balaam," said Mr. Cozart, "this baby will be your master. I want you to look after him and take care of him."

"Yes, suh," said Balaam, regarding his

new master with both interest and curiosity. "He look like he older dan w'at he is." With that Balaam retreated to the negro quarters, where he had a strange tale to tell the other children about the new white baby.

Berrien grew and thrived, and when he was a year old Balaam took charge of him, and the two soon became devoted to each other. The negro would take the child on his back and carry him from one end of the plantation to the other, and Berrien was never happy unless Balaam was somewhere in sight. Once, when it was found necessary to correct Balaam with a switch for some boyish offense, his young master fell on the floor in a convulsion of rage and grief. This manifestation made such an impression on the family that no further attempt was ever made to punish Balaam; and so the two grew up together — the young master with a temper of extreme violence and an obstinacy that had no bounds, and the negro with an independence and a fearlessness extremely rare among slaves.

It was observed by all, and was a cause of special wonder among the negroes, that, in spite of Berrien Cozart's violent temper, he never turned his hand against Balaam, not even when he was too young to reason about the matter. Sometimes, when he was seen throwing stones in a peculiarly vicious way at a tree, or at the chickens, or at some of the other children, the older negroes would laughingly shake their heads at one another and say that the child was mad with Balaam.

These queer relations between master and slave grew stronger as the two grew older. When Berrien was ten and Balaam twenty they were even more inseparable than they had been when the negro was trudging about the plantation with his young master on his back. At that time Balaam was not allowed to sleep in the big house; but when Berrien was ten he had a room to himself, and the negro slept on a pallet by the side of the bed.

About this time it was thought necessary to get a private tutor for Berrien. He had a great knack for books in a fitful sort of way, but somehow the tutor, who was an estimable young gentleman from Philadelphia, was not very much to Berrien's taste. For a day or two matters went along smoothly enough, but it was not long before Balaam, lying on the floor outside the door, heard a tremendous racket and clatter in the room. Looking in, he saw his young master pelting the tutor with books and using language that was far from polite. Balaam went in, closing the door carefully behind him, and almost immediately the tumult ceased. Then the negro appeared leading his young master by the arm. They went downstairs and out on the lawn. The tutor, perplexed and astonished by the fierce temper of his pupil, saw the two from the window and watched them curiously. Berrien finally stopped and leaned against a tree. The negro, with his hand on the boy's shoulder, was saying something unpleasant, for the tutor observed one or two fierce gestures of protest. But these soon ceased, and presently Berrien walked rapidly back to the house, followed by Balaam. The tutor heard them coming up the stairway; then the door opened, and his pupil entered and apologized for his rudeness.

For some time there was such marked improvement in Berrien's behavior that his tutor often wondered what influence the negro had brought to bear on his young master; but he never found out. In fact, he soon forgot all about the matter, for the improvement was only temporary. The youngster became so disagreeable and so unmanageable that the tutor was glad to give up his position at the end of the year. After that Berrien was sent to the Academy, and there he made considerable progress, for he was spurred on in his studies by the example of the other boys. But he was a wild youth, and there was no mischief, no matter how malicious it might be, in which he was not the leader. As his character unfolded itself the fact became more and more manifest that he had an unsavory career before him. Some of the older heads predicted that he would come to the gallows, and there was certainly some ground for these gloomy suggestions, for never before had the quiet community of Billville given development to such reckless wickedness as that which marked the daily life of Berrien Cozart as he grew older. Sensual, cruel, impetuous, and implacable, he was the wonder of the mild-mannered people of the county, and a terror to the God-fearing. Nevertheless, he was attractive even to those who regarded him as the imp of the Evil One, and many a love-lorn maiden was haunted by his beautiful face in her dreams.

When Berrien was eighteen he was sent to Franklin College at Athens, which was supposed to divide the responsibility of guardianship with a student's parents. The atmosphere the young man found there in those days suited him admirably. He became the leader of the wildest set at that venerable institution, and proceeded to make a name for himself as the promoter and organizer of the most disreputable escapades the college had ever known. He was an aggressor in innumerable broils, he fought a duel in the suburbs of Athens, and he ended his college career by insulting the chancellor in the lecture-room. He was expelled, and the students and the people of Athens breathed freer when it was known that he had gone home never to return.

There was a curious scene with his father when the wayward youth returned to Billville in disgrace. The people of that town had received some inkling of the sort of education the young man was getting at college, though Mr. Cozart was inclined to look somewhat leniently on the pranks of son, ascribing them to the hot blood of youth. But when Berrien's creditors began to send in their accounts, amounting to several thousands of dollars, he realized for the first time that the hope and pride of his later years had been vain delusions. Upon the heels of the accounts came Berrien himself, handsomer and more attractive than ever. Dissipation was not one of his vices, and he returned with the bloom of youth on his cheek and the glowing fires of health in his sparkling eyes. He told the story of his expulsion with an air as gay as any cavalier ever assumed. The story was told at the table, and there was company present. But this fact was ignored by Berrien's father. His hand shook as he laid down his knife and fork.

"You have damaged my credit," he said to his son across the table; "you have disgraced your mother's name and mine; and now you have the impudence to make a joke of it at my table, sir. Let me not see your face in this house again until you have returned to college and wiped out the blot you have placed on your name."

"As you please, sir," said Berrien. His eyes were still full of laughter, but some of those who were at the table said his nether lip trembled a little. He rose, bowed, and passed out.

Balaam was in his young master's room when the latter went in. He had unpacked the trunk and the valise and was placing the things in a clothes-press, meanwhile talking with himself, as most negroes will when left to themselves. Berrien entered, humming the tune of a college glee.

"I 'lowed you was at dinner, Marse Berry," said Balaam.

"I have finished," said young Cozart. "Have you had yours?"

"Lord! no, suh. Hit 'll be 'way yander todes night 'fo' I kin git dese clo'es straightened out."

"Well," said the young man, "you go and get your dinner as soon as you can. This valise must be repacked. Before the sun goes down we must be away from here."

"Good Lord, Marse Berry! I ain't said howdy wid none er de folks yit. How come we got ter go right off?"

"You can stay, if you choose," said Berrien. "I reckon you 'd be a better negro if you had stayed at home all the time. Right now you ought to be picking your five hundred pounds of cotton every day."

"Now, you know, Marse Berry, dat of you er gwine, I 'm gwine too — you know dat p'intedly; but you come in on me so sudden-like dat you sorter git me flustrated."

"Well," said Berrien, seating himself on the side of the bed and running his fingers through his curling hair, "if you go with me this time you will be taking a big jump in the dark. There's no telling where you'll land. Pap has taken the studs, and I have made up my mind to leave here for good and all. You belong to me, but I'll give you your choice; you can go with me, or you can stay. If you go, I'll probably get into a tight place and sell you; if you stay, Pap will make a pet of you for my sake."

Regarding this as a very good offhand joke, the young man laughed so loud that the sound of it penetrated to the dining-room, and, mellow and hearty as it was, it struck strangely on the ears of those still sitting at the table.

"I knowed in reason dat dey was gwine to be a rippit," said Balaam; "kaze you know how you been gwine on up yander, Marse Berry. I tole an' tole you 'bout it, an' I dunno whar in de name' er goodness you'd been ef I had n't been right dar fer ter look atter you."

"Yes," remarked Berrien, sarcastically, "you were just about drunk enough half the time to look after me like a Dutch uncle."

Balaam held his head down and chuckled. "Yes, suh," he said, "I tuck my dram, dey ain't no 'sputin' er dat; yit I never has tuck so much dat I ain't keep my eye on you. But 't ain't do no good: you des went right 'long; an' dar was ole Mistiss, which she done sick in bed, an' Miss Sally Carter, which she 's yo' born cousin — dar dey all was a-specktin' you ter head de whole school gang. An' you did head 'em, mon, but not in de books."

"My fair Cousin Sarah!" exclaimed Berrien in a reminiscent way.

"Yes, suh," said Balaam; "an' dey tells me down in de kitchen dat she comin' yere dis ve'y day."

"Then," said the young man, "it is time for me to be going. Get your dinner. If I am to have your company, you must be ready in an hour; if you want to stay, go to the overseer and tell him to put you to work."

Laughing good-naturedly, Balaam slipped out. After a little while Berrien Cozart went down the stairway and into the room of his mother, who was an invalid. He sat at her bedside and talked a few moments. Then he straightened and smoothed her pillows, stroked her gray hair, gazed into her gentle eyes, and kissed her twice. These things the poor lady remembered long afterwards. Straying into the spacious parlor, the young man looked around on the familiar furniture and the walls covered with portraits. Prominent among these was the beautiful face of Sally Carter. The red curtains in the windows, swaying to and fro in the wind, so swiftly changed the light and shadow that the fair face in the heavy gilt frame seemed to be charged with life. The lustrous eyes seemed to dance and the saucy lips to smile. Berrien remembered his fair cousin with pleasure. She had been his playmate when he was younger, and the impression she made on him had been a lasting one. Beautiful as she was, there was no nonsense about her. She was high-spirited and jolly, and the young man smiled as he recalled some of their escapades together. He raised his hand to salute the portrait, and at that moment a peal of merry laughter greeted his ears. Turning, he saw framed in the doorway the rosy original of the portrait. Before he could recover from his astonishment the young lady had seized and kissed him. Then she held him off at arm's length and looked at him.

"Why, how handsome you have grown;" she cried. "Just think of it! I expected to meet a regular border ruffian. My dear boy, you have no idea what a tremendous reputation your friends have given you. Ann Burney — you remember that funny little creature, don't you? as fat as a butterball — Ann told me the other day that you were positively the terror of everybody around Athens. And now I find you here kissing your fingers at my portrait on the wall. I declare, it is too romantic for anything! After this I know you will never call me Sarah Jane."

"You have taken me by surprise," said Berrien, as soon as he could get in a word. "I was admiring the skill of the artist. The lace there, falling against the velvet bodice, is neatly done."

"Ah, but you are blushing; you are confused!" exclaimed Miss Carter. "You have n't even told me you are glad to see me."

"There is no need to tell you that," said Berrien. "I was just thinking, when you rushed in on me, how good and kind you always were. You are maturer than the portrait there, but you are more beautiful."

Miss Carter bent low with a mock courtesy, but the color in her face was warmer as she exclaimed: —

"Oh, how nice you are! The portrait there is only sixteen, and I am twenty-five. Just think of that! And just think of me at that age — what a tomboy I was! But I must run and tell the rest of the folks howdy."

Berrien Cozart walked out on the veranda, and presently he was joined by his father. "My son," said the old gentleman, "you will need money for your traveling expenses. Here is a check on our Augusta factor; you can have it cashed in Madison. I want you to return to college, make all proper apologies, and redeem yourself."

"Thank you, sir," said Berrien, taking the check and stuffing it into his pocket. His father turned to go indoors, hesitated a moment, and looked at Berrien, who was drumming idly on one of the pillars. Then the old gentleman sighed and went in.

Shortly thereafter Berrien Cozart and Balaam were journeying away from Billville in the conveyance that had brought them there.

On the high hill beyond the "town branch" Balaam leaned out of the hack and looked back at Billville. The town appeared insignificant enough; but the setting sun imparted a rosy glow to the roof of the yellow court-house and to the spire of the old church. Observing the purpose of the negro, Mr. Cozart smiled cynically and flipped the hot ashes of his cigar into Balaam's ear.

"As you are telling the town good-by," said the young man, "I'll help you to bow."

"Yasser!" said Balaam, shaking the ashes from his ear; "I was des a-lookin' back at de place. Dat sun shine red, mon, an' de jail look like she de bigges' house dar. She stan' out mo' bigger dan w'at de chu'ch do."

It may be that this statement made no impression on Berrien, but he leaned back in his seat and for miles chewed the end of his cigar in silence.

It is not the purpose of this chronicle to follow him through all his adventures and escapades. As he rode away from Billville on that memorable day he seemed to realize that his career had just begun. It was a career to which he had served a long and faithful apprenticeship, and he pursued it to the end. From Madison he went to Atlanta, where for months he was a familiar, albeit a striking figure. There were few games of chance in which he was not an adept. No conjurer was so adroit with the cards or the dice; he handled these emblems of fate and disaster as an artist handles his tools. And luck chose him as her favorite; he prospered to such a degree that he grew reckless and careless. Whereupon one fine day luck turned her back on him, and he paraded on fine afternoons in front of Lloyd's Hotel a penniless man. He had borrowed and lost until he could borrow no longer.

Balaam, who was familiar with the situation, was not surprised to learn that his master had made up his mind to sell him.

"Well, suh," said Balaam, brushing his master's coat carefully, "you kin sell me, but de man dat buys Balaam will git a mighty bad bargain."

"What do you mean?" exclaimed Berrien.

"You kin sell me, suh, but I ain't gwine stay wid um."

"You can't help yourself," said the master.

"I got legs, Marse Berry. You know dat yo'se'f."

"Your legs will do you no good. You'll be caught if you go back home."

"I ain't gwine dar, suh. I'm gwine wid you. I hear you say yistiddy night p'intedly dat you gwine 'way f'om dis place, an' I'm gwine wid you. I been 'long wid you all de time, an' ole marster done tole me w'en you was baby dat I got ter stay wid you."

Something in this view seemed to strike Mr. Cozart. He walked up and down the floor a few minutes, and then fell to laughing.

"By George, Balaam, you are a trump, — a royal flush in spades. It will be a famous joke."

Thereupon Berrien Cozart arranged his cards, so to speak, for a more hazardous game than any he had ever yet played. He went with Balaam to a trader who was an expert in the slave market, and who knew its ups and downs, its weak points and its strong points. At first Berrien was disposed to put Balaam on the block and have him auctioned off to the highest bidder; but the trader knew the negro, and had already made a study of his strong points. To be perfectly sure, however, he thumped Balaam on the chest, listened to the beating of his heart, and felt of his muscles in quite a professional way.

"I reckon he ain't noways vicious," said the trader, looking at Balaam's smiling face.

"I have never seen him angry or sullen," said Mr. Cozart. Other questions were asked, and finally the trader jotted down this memorandum in his note-book: —

"Buck nigger, Balaam; age 32; 6 feet 1 inch; sound as a dollar; see Colonel Strother."

Then the trader made an appointment with Berrien for the next day, and said he thought the negro could be disposed off at private sale. Such was the fact, for when Berrien went back the next day the trader met him with an offer of fifteen hundred dollars in cash for Balaam.

"Make it eighteen," said Mr. Cozart.

"Well, I'll tell you what I'll do," said the trader, closing his eyes and pursing his mouth in a business-like way. "I'll give you sixteen fifty — no more, no less. Come, now, that's fair. Split the difference."

Thereupon Mr. Cozart said it was a bargain, and the trader paid him the money down after the necessary papers were drawn up. Balaam seemed to be perfectly satisfied. All he wanted, he said, was to have a master who would treat him well. He went with Berrien to the hotel to fetch his little belongings, and if the trader had searched him when he returned he would have found strapped around his body a belt containing fifty dollars in specie.

Having thus, in a manner, replenished his empty purse, Mr. Berrien Cozart made haste to change his field of operations. To his competitors in his own special department of industry he let drop the hint that he was going to Columbus, and thence to Mobile and New Orleans, where he would hang on the outskirts of the racing season, picking up such crumbs and contributions as might naturally fall in the way of a professional gentleman who kept his eyes open and his fingers nimble enough to deal himself a winning hand.

As a matter of fact Mr. Cozart went to Nashville, and he had not been gone many days before Balaam disappeared. He had been missing two days before Colonel Strother, his new master, took any decided action, but on the morning of the fourth day the following advertisement appeared among others of a like character in the columns of the Atlanta " Intelligencer " : —

$100 reward will be paid for the apprehension of my negro boy *Balaam*. Thirty-odd years old, but appeared younger; tall, pleasant-looking, quick-spoken, and polite. Was formerly the property of the Hon. William Cozart. He is supposed to be making his way to his old home. Was well dressed when last seen. Milledgeville " Recorder " and " Federal Union " please copy.

BOZEMAN STROTHER,
Atlanta, Georgia.

(d. & w. 1 mo.)

This advertisement duly appeared in the Milledgeville papers, which were published not far from Billville, but no response was ever made; the reward was never claimed. Considering the strength and completeness of the patrol system of that day, Balaam's adventure was a risky one; but, fortunately for him, a wiser head than his had planned his flight and instructed him thoroughly in the part he was to play. The shrewdness of

Berrien Cozart had provided against all difficulties. Balaam left Atlanta at night, but he did not go as a fugitive. He was armed with a "pass" which formally set forth to all to whom it might concern that the boy David had express permission to join his master in Nashville, and this "pass" bore the signature of Elmore Avery, a gentleman who existed only in the imagination of Mr. Berrien Cozart. Attached thereto, also, was the signature seal of the judge of ordinary. With this little document Balaam would have found no difficulty whatever in traveling. The people he met would have reasoned that the negro whose master trusted him to make so long a journey alone must be an uncommonly faithful one, but Balaam met with an adventure that helped him along much more comfortably than the pass could have helped him. It is best, perhaps, to tell the story in his own language, as he told it long afterwards.

"I won't say I were n't skeered," said Balaam, "kaze I was; yit I were n't skeered 'nough fer ter go slippin' 'longside er de fences an' 'mongst de pine thickets. I des kep' right in de big road. Atter I got out er town a little piece, I tuck off my shoes an' tied de strings tergedder an' slung 'em 'cross my shoulder, on top my satchel, an' den I sorter mended my gait. I struck up a kind er dog-trot, an' by de time day come a many a mile lay 'twix' me an' Atlanta. Little atter sun-up I hear some horses trottin' on de road de way I come, an' bimeby a man driv up in a double buggy. He say, 'Hello, boy! Whar you gwine?' I pulled off my hat, an' say, 'I gwine whar my marster is, suh.' Den de white man 'low, 'W'at he name?' Well, suh, when de man ax me dat, hit come over me like a big streak er de chill an' fever dat I done clean fergit de name what Marse Berry choosen ter be call by. So I des runned my han' und' de lindin' er my hat an' pulled out de pass, an' say, 'Boss, dis piece er paper kin talk lots better dan I kin.'

"De man look at me right hard, an' den he tuck de pass an' read it out loud. Well, suh, w'en he come ter de name I des grabbed holt un it wid my min', an' I ain't never turned it loose tell yit. De man was drivin' long slow, an' I was walkin' by de buggy. He helt de pass in his han's some little time, den he look at me an' scratch his head. Atter a while he 'low: 'You got a mighty long journey befo' you. Kin you drive? Ef you kin, put on yo' shoes an' mount up here an' take dese lines.'

"Well, suh, I wuz sorter glad, an' yit I wuz sorter skittish, but I tol' de white man thankydo, an' le'pt up in dat buggy like I was de gladdes' nigger in de worl'. De man he keep on lookin' at me, an' bimeby he say, 'I tuck a notion when I fust see you dat you was de boy w'at Cozart had in Atlanta.' Mon! you could er knocked me over wid a feather, I was dat weak; but I bu'st out laughin' an' 'low, 'Lord, boss! ef I wa' n't no better lookin' dan dat ar Cozart nigger I'd quit bein' a nigger an' take up wid de monkey tribe.' De man say, 'I had de idee dat de Cozart nigger was a mighty likely boy. What was his name? Balaam?' I was so skeered it fair make me sick at de stomach, yit I talk right out. I 'low, 'Dey call 'im Balaam, an' dey have ter whale 'im.' De man he laugh, 'He got a great big scyar on de side er his neck now whar somebody hit 'im a diff, an' he lay roun' dem hotels an' drink dram all night long.' De man look sideways at my neck. 'Dat nigger got so bad dat his marster had ter sell 'im, an' dey tells me, suh, dat de man w'at buy 'im ain' no mo' dan paid de money fer 'im dan he have ter take 'im down and strop 'im.'

"Well, suh, de man look at me an laugh so funny dat it make my ve'y limbs ache. Yes, suh. My heart hit up 'g'inst my ribs des like a flutter-mill; an' I wuz so skeered it make my tongue run slicker dan sin. He ax me mo' questions dan I could answer now, but I made answer den des like snappin' my fingers. W'at make me de mo' skeered was de way dat ar white man done. He 'd look at me an' laugh, an' de plumper I gin 'im de answer de mo' he 'd laugh. I say ter myse'f, I did: 'Balaam, you 'r' a goner, dat w'at you is. De man know you, an' de fust calaboose he come ter he gwine slap you in dar.' I had a mighty good notion ter jump out er dat buggy an' make a break fer de woods, but stidder dat I sot right whar I wuz, kaze I knowed in reason dat ef de man want me right bad an' I wuz ter break an' run he 'd fetch me down wid a pistol.

"Well, suh, dat man joke an' laugh de whole blessed mornin,' an' den bimeby we drove in a town not much bigger dan Bivvle" (which was Balaam's pet name for Billville), "an' dar de white man say we 'd stop fer dinner. He ain't say de word too soon fer me, mon, kaze I was so hongry an' tired it make my head swim. We driv up ter tavern, we did, an' de folks dar dey holler, 'Howdy, Judge,' an' de white man he holler 'Howdy' back, an' den he tol' me ter take de horses an' buggy down ter de liberty stable an' have 'em fed, an' den come back an' git my dinner. Dat wuz mighty good news; but whilst I wuz eatin' my dinner I hear dat white man laughin', an' it come over me dat he know who I wuz an' dat he wuz gwine ter gi' me up; yit dat ain't hender my appetite, an' I des sot dar an' stuff myse'f tell I des make de yuther niggers open der eyes. An' den, when I git my belly full, I sot in de sun an' went right fast ter sleep. I 'spec' I tuck a right smart nap, kaze when some un hollered at me an' woke me up de sun wuz gwine down de hill right smartly. I jumped up on my feet, I did, an' I say, 'Who dat callin' me?' Somebody 'low, 'Yo' marster want you.' Den I bawl out, 'Is Marse Berry come?' De niggers all laugh, an' one un 'em say, 'Dat nigger man dreamin', mon. He ain't woke good yit.'

"By dat time I done come ter my senses,

an' den I ax dem wharbouts marster is. Bimeby, when I done foun' de white man w'at bring me in his buggy, he look at me sorter funny an' say, 'You know whar you lef' my buggy: well, you go down an' raise up de seat an' fetch me de little box you 'll fin' in dar. Wrop it up in de buggy rug an' fetch it an' put it on de table dar.' Well, suh, I went an' got dat box, an' time I put my han' on it I knowed des 'zactly w'at wuz on de inside er it. I done seed too many er 'em. It wuz under lock an' key, but I knowed it wuz a farrar box like dem w'at Marse Berry done his gamblin' wid. By de time I got back ter de room in de tavern de white man done had de table kivered wid a piece er cloff w'at he got out 'n his satchel. He tuck de box, onlocked it, rattled de chips in his han', an' shuffled de kyards. Den he look at me an' laugh. He was de quarest white man dat ever I laid eyes on.

"Atter while I ax 'im ef I had n't better be gitten' 'long todes de eend er my journey. He 'low: 'Lord, no! I want you ter set round yere atter supper an' gi' me luck. You ain't losin' no time, kaze I 'm a-gwine plumb to Chattanoogy, an' ef you 'll be ez spry ez you kin be I 'll take you 'long wid me.' De ups an' odds er it was dat I stayed wid de man. De folks named 'im Judge, an' he was a judge, mon. 'Long 'bout nine dat night he come ter his room, whar I was waitin' fer 'im, an' soon atter dat de young gentlemens 'bout town 'gun ter drap in, an' 't wa'n't long 'fo' de game got started. Look like de man ain't wanter play, but de yuthers dey kep' on coaxin', an' presently he fotch out de box an' opened up. Well, sah, I done seed lots er gamblin' fust an' last, but dat white man beat my time. Dey played poker, stidder farrar, an' it look like ter me dat de man done got de kyards trained. He dealt 'em 'boveboard, an' dey des come in his han' 'zackly like he want 'em ter come. Ef he had any tricks like w'at Marse Berry played on folks, dey was too slick fer my eye, yit he des beated dem yuther mens scand'lous. It was des like one er dese yere great big river cats ketchin' minners.

"Atter dey been playin' some little time, de white man what brung me dar 'low: 'Boy, you better go git some sleep. We'll start soon in de mornin'.' But I say, 'No, suh; I'll des set in de cornder here an' nod, an' I'll be close by ef so be you want me.' I sot dar, I did, an' I had a good chance ter sleep, kaze, bless yo' heart! dem mens ain't make much fuss. Dey des grip der kyards an' sorter hol' der bref. Sometimes one un 'em would break out an' cuss a word er two, but inginer'lly dey 'd plank up der scads an' lose 'em des like dey wuz usen ter it. De white man w'at dey call Judge he des wiped 'em up, an' at de een' he wuz des ez fresh ez he wuz at de start. It wuz so nigh day when de game broke up dat Marse Judge 'lowed dat it was too late fer supper an' not quite soon 'nough fer breakfas', an' den he say he wuz gwine ter take a walk an' git some a'r.

"Well, suh, it wuz dat away all de time I wuz wid dat white man — laughin' an' jokin' all day, an' gamblin' all night long. How an' when he got sleep I 'll never tell you, kaze he wuz wide awake eve'y time I seed 'im. It went on dis away plumb till we got ter de Tennessy River, dar whar Chattynoogy is. Atter we sorter rested, de white man tuck me 'cross de river, an' we druv on ter whar de stage changes hosses. Dar we stopped, an' whilst I wuz waitin' fer de stage de white man 'low, 'Balaam!' He kotch me so quick, dat I jump des like I 'd been shot, an' hollered out, 'Suh!' Den he laugh sorter funny, an' say: 'Don't look skeered, Balaam; I knowed you fum de off-start. You 'r' a mighty good boy, but yo' marster is a borned rascal. I 'm gwine send you whar you say he is, an' I want you ter tell 'im dis fum me — dat dough he tried ter rob me, yit fer de sake er his Cousin Sally, I he'ped you ter go whar he is.'

"Den de man got in his buggy an' driv back, an' dat de las' time I ever laid eyes on 'im. When de stage come 'long I got up wid de driver, an' 't wa'n't long 'fo' I wuz wid Marse Berry, an' I ain't no sooner seed 'im dan I knowed he was gwine wrong wuss and wuss: not but w'at he was glad kaze I come, but it look like his face done got mo' harder. Well, suh, it was des dat away. I ain't gwine ter tell you all w'at he done an' how he done it, kaze he was my own marster, an' he never hit me a lick amiss, 'ceppin' it was when he was a little boy. I ain't gwine ter tell you whar we went an' how we got dar, kaze dey done been too much talk now. But we drapped down inter Alabam', an' den inter Massasip', an' den inter Arkansaw, an' back ag'in inter Massasip'; an' one night whilst we wuz on one er dem big river boats, Marse Berry he got inter a mighty big row. Dey wuz playin' kyards fer de bigges' kind er stakes, an' fust news I know de lie was passed, an' den de whole gang made fer Marse Berry. Dey whipped out der knives an' der pistols, an' it look like it wuz gwine ter be all night wid Marse Berry. Well, suh, I got so skeered dat I picked up a cheer an' smashed de nighest man, and by dat time Marse Berry had shot one; an', suh, we des cleaned 'em out. Den Marse Berry made a dash fer de low'-mos' deck, an' I dashed atter 'im. Den I hear sumpin' go ker-slosh in de water, an' I 'lowed it was Marse Berry, an' in I splunged head-foremos'. An' den — but, Lord, suh, you know de balance des good ez I does, kaze I hear tell dat dey wuz sumpin' n'er 'bout it in de papers."

This was as far as Balaam ever would go with the story of his adventure. He had made a hero of Berrien Cozart from his youth, and he refused to dwell on any episode in the young man's career that, to his mind, was not worthy of a Cozart. When Berrien leaped to the lower deck of the steamboat his foot touched a stick of wood. This he flung into the river, and then hid himself among the cotton bales that were piled on the forward part of the boat. It will never be known whether he threw the piece of wood into the water knowing that Balaam would follow, or whether his sole intention was to elude pursuit. A shot or two was fired, but the bullets fell wide of their mark, and the boat swept on, leaving the negro swimming around, searching for his master.

At the next landing-place Berrien slipped ashore unseen. But fortune no longer favored him; for the next day a gentleman who had been a passenger on the boat recognized him, and an attempt was made to arrest him. He shot the high sheriff of the county through the head, and became a fugitive indeed. He was pursued through Alabama into Georgia, and being finally captured not a mile away from Billville, was thrown into jail in the town where he was born. His arrest, owing to the standing of his family, created a tremendous sensation in the quiet village. Before he was carried to jail he asked that his father be sent for. The messenger tarried some little time, but he returned alone.

"What did my father say?" Berrien asked with some eagerness.

"He said," replied the messenger, "that he did n't want to see you."

"Did he write that message?" the young man inquired.

"Oh, no!" the messenger declared. "He just waved his arm — so — and said he did n't want to see you."

At once the troubled expression on Berrien Cozart's face disappeared. He looked around on the crowd and smiled.

"You see what it is," he said with a light laugh, "to be the pride of a family! Gentlemen, I am ready. Don't let me keep you waiting." And so, followed by half the population of his native village, he was escorted to jail.

This building was a two-story brick structure, as solid as good material and good work could make it, and there was no fear that any prisoner could escape, especially from the dungeon where Berrien's captors insisted on confining him. Nevertheless the jailer was warned to take unusual precautions. This official, however, who occupied with his family the first story of the jail, merely smiled. He had grown old in the business of keeping this jail, and certainly he knew a great deal more about it than those Mississippi officials who were strutting around and putting on such airs.

To his other duties the jailer added those of tyler of the little lodge of freemasons that had its headquarters in a hall on the public square, and it so happened that the lodge was to meet on the very night that Berrien was put into jail. After supper the jailer, as had been his habit for years, smoked his pipe, and then went down to the village and lighted the lamps in the masonic hall. His wife and daughter, full of the subject of Berrien Cozart's imprisonment, went to a neighbor's not far away for the purpose of discussing the matter. As they passed out of the gate they heard the jailer blowing the tin trumpet which was the signal for the masons to assemble.

It was nearly eleven o'clock when the jailer returned, but he found his wife and daughter waiting for him. Both had a troubled air, and they lost no time in declaring that they had heard weeping and sobbing upstairs in the dungeon. The jailer himself was very sympathetic, having known Berrien for many years, and he took another turn at his pipe by way of consolation. Then, as was his custom, he took his lantern and went around the jail on a tour of inspection to see that everything was safe.

He did not go far. First he stumbled over a pile of bricks, and then his shoulder struck a ladder. He uttered a little cry and looked upward, and there, dim as his lantern was, he could see a black and gaping hole in the wall of the dungeon. He ran into the house as fast as his rheumatic legs could carry him, and he screamed to his wife and daughter: —

"Raise the alarm! Cozart has escaped! We are ruined!"

Then he ran to the dungeon door, flung it open, and then fell back with a cry of terror. What did he see, and what did the others who joined him there see? On the floor lay Berrien Cozart dead, and crouching beside him was Balaam. How the negro had managed to make his way through the masonry of the dungeon without discovery is still one of the mysteries of Billville. But, prompt as he was, he was too late. His master had escaped through a wider door. He had made his way to a higher court. Death, coming to him in that dark dungeon, must have visited him in the similitude of a happy dream, for there under the light of the lanterns he lay smiling sweetly as a little child that nestles on its mother's breast; and on the floor near him, where it had dropped from his nerveless hand, was a golden locket, from which smiled the lovely face of Sally Carter.

A CONSCRIPT'S CHRISTMAS.

On a Sunday afternoon in December, 1863, two horsemen were making their way across Big Corn Valley in the direction of Sugar Mountain. They had started from the little town of Jasper early in the morning, and it was apparent at a glance that they had not enjoyed the journey. They sat listlessly in their saddles, with their carbines across their laps, and whatever conversation they carried on was desultory.

To tell the truth, the journey from Jasper to the top of Sugar Mountain was not a pleasant one even in the best of weather, and now, with the wind pushing before it a bitterly cold mist, its disagreeableness was irritating. And it was not by any means a short journey. Big Corn Valley was fifteen miles across as the crow flies, and the meanderings of the road added five more. Then there was the barrier of the foothills, and finally Sugar Mountain itself, which when the weather was clear lifted itself above all the other mountains of that region.

Nor was this all. Occasionally, when the wind blew aside the oilskin overcoats of the riders, the gray uniform of the Confederacy showed beneath, and they wore cavalry boots, and there were tell-tale trimmings on their felt hats. With these accoutrements to advertise them, they were not in a friendly region. There were bushwhackers in the mountains, and, for aught the horsemen knew, the fodder stacks in the valley, that rose like huge and ominous ghosts out of the mist on every side, might conceal dozens of guerrillas. They had that day ridden past the house of the only member of the Georgia State convention who had refused to affix his signature to the ordinance of secession, and the woods, to use the provincial phrase, were full of Union men.

Suddenly, and with a fierce and ripping oath, one of the horsemen drew rein. "I wish I may die," he exclaimed, his voice trembling with long pent up irritation, "if I ain't a great mind to turn around in my tracks an' go back. Where does this cussed road lead to anyhow?"

"To the mountain — straight to the mountain," grimly remarked the other, who had stopped to see what was the matter with his companion.

"Great Jerusalem! straight? Do you see that fodder stack yonder with the hawk on the top of the pole? Well, we've passed it four times, and we ain't no further away from it now than we was at fust."

"Well, we've no time to stand here. In an hour we'll be at the foot of the mountain, and a quarter of a mile further we'll find shelter. We must attend to business and talk it over afterwards."

"An' it's a mighty nice business, too," said the man who had first spoken. He was slender in build, and his thin and straggling mustache failed to relieve his effeminate appearance. He had evidently never seen hard service. "I never have believed in this conscriptin' business," he went on in a complaining tone. "It won't pan out. It has turned more men agin the Confederacy than it has turned fer it, or else my daddy's name ain't Bill Chadwick, nor mine neither."

"Well," said the other curtly, "it's the law, Bill Chadwick, and it must be carried out. We've got our orders."

"Oh, yes! You are the commander,

Cap'n Moseley, an' I 'm the army. Ain't I the gayest army you ever had under you? I 'll tell you what, Cap'n Moseley (I 'd call you Dick, like I useter, if we was n't in the ranks), when I j'ined the army I thought I was goin' to fight the Yankees, but they slapped me in the camp of instruction over there at Adairsville, an' now here we are fightin' our own folks. If we ain't fightin' 'em, we are pursuin' after 'em, an' runnin' 'em into the woods an' up the mountains. Now what kind of a soldier will one of these conscripts make? You need n't tell me, Cap'n! The law won't pan out."

"But it 's the law," said Captain Moseley. The captain had been wounded in Virginia, and was entitled to a discharge, but he accepted the position of conscript officer. He had the grit and discipline of a veteran, and a persistence in carrying out his purposes that gave him the name of "Hardhead" in the army. He was tall and muscular, but his drooping left shoulder showed where a Federal bullet had found lodgment. His closely cropped beard was slightly streaked with gray, and his face would have been handsome had not determination left its rude handwriting there.

The two rode on together in silence a little space, the cold mists, driven by the wind, tingling in their faces. Presently Private Chadwick, who had evidently been ruminating over the matter, resumed the thread of his complaints.

"They tell me," he said, "that it's a heap easier to make a bad law than it is to make a good one. It takes a lot of smart men a long time to make a good one, but a passel of blunderbusses can patch a bad one up in a little or no time. That's the way I look at it.

"What's the name of this chap we are after? Israel Spurlock? I'd like to know, by George, what's the matter with him! What makes him so plague-taked important that two men have to be sent on a wild-goose chase after him? They yerked him into army, an' he yerked himself out, an' now the word is that the war can't go on unless Israel Spurlock is on hand to fling down his gun an' run when he hears a bung-shell playin' a tune in the air."

Captain Moseley coughed to hide a smile.

"It's jest like I tell you, Cap'n. The news is that we had a terrible victory at Chattanooga, but I notice in the Atlanta papers that the Yankees ain't no further north than they was before the fight; an' what makes it wuss, they are warmin' themselves in Chattanooga, whilst we are shiverin' outside. I reckon if Israel Spurlock had been on hand at the right time an' in the right place, we'd a drove the Yanks plumb back to Nashville. Lord! I hope we'll have him on the skirmish line the next time we surround the enemy an' drive him into a town as big as Chattanooga."

Private Chadwick kept up his complaints for some time, but they failed to disturb the serenity of the captain, who urged his horse forward through the mist, closely followed by his companion. They finally left the valley, passed over the foothills, and began the ascent of Sugar Mountain. Here their journey became less disagreeable. The road, winding and twisting around the mountain, had been cut through a dense growth of trees, and these proved to be something of a shelter. Moreover, the road sometimes brought the mountain between the travelers and the wind, and these were such comfortable intervals that Mr. Chadwick ceased his complaints and rode along good-humoredly.

The two horsemen had gone about a

mile, measuring the mountain road, though they were not more than a quarter of a mile from the foot, when they came suddenly on an old man sitting in a sheltered place by the side of the road. They came on the stranger so suddenly that their horses betrayed alarm, and it was all they could do to keep the animals from slipping and rolling into the gorge at their left. The old man was dressed in a suit of gray jeans, and wore a wool hat, which, although it showed the signs of constant use, had somehow managed to retain its original shape. His head was large and covered with a profusion of iron-gray hair, which was neatly combed. His face was round, but the lines of character obliterated all suggestions of chubbiness. The full beard that he wore failed to hide evidences of firmness and determination; but around his mouth a serene smile lingered, and humor sparkled in his small brown eyes.

"Howdy, boys, howdy!" he exclaimed. "Tired as they look to be, you er straddlin' right peart creeturs. A flirt or two more an' they'd 'a' flung you down the hill, an' 'a' follered along atter you, headstall an' stirrup. They done like they were n't expectin' company in an' around here."

The sonorous voice and deliberate utterance of the old man bespoke his calling. He was evidently a minister of the gospel. This gave a clew to Captain Moseley's memory.

"This must be Uncle Billy Powers," said the captain. "I have heard you preach many a time when I was a boy."

"That's my name," said Uncle Billy; "an' in my feeble way I've been a-preachin' the Word as it was given to me forty year, lackin' one. Ef I ever saw you, the circumstance has slipped from me."

"My name is Moseley," said the captain.

"I useter know Jeremiah Moseley in my younger days," said Uncle Billy, gazing reflectively at the piece of pine bark he was whittling. "Yes, yes! I knowed Brother Moseley well. He was a God-fearin' man."

"He was my father," said the captain.

"Well, well, well!" exclaimed Uncle Billy, in a tone that seemed to combine reflection with astonishment. "Jerry Moseley's son; I disremember the day when Brother Moseley came into my mind, an' yit, now that I hear his name bandied about up here on the hill, it carries me back to ole times. He weren't much of a preacher on his own hook, but let 'im foller along for to clench the sermon, an' his match could n't be foun' in them days. Yit, Jerry was a man of peace, an' here's his son a-gwine about with guns an' pistols, an' what not, a-tryin' to give peaceable folks a smell of war."

"Oh, no!" said Captain Moseley, laughing; "we are just hunting up some old acquaintances, — some friends of ours that we'd like to see."

"Well," said Uncle Billy, sinking his knife deep into the soft pine bark, "it's bad weather for a frolic, an' it ain't much better for a straight-out, eve'y-day call. Speshually up here on the hill, where the ground is so wet and slipperyfied. It looks like you've come a mighty long ways for to pay a friendly call. An' yit," the old man continued, looking up at the captain with a smile that well became his patriarchal face, "thar ain't a cabin on the hill whar you won't be more than welcome. Yes, sir; wheresomever you find a h'a'thstone, thar you'll find a place to rest."

"So I have heard," said the captain. "But maybe you can cut our journey short. We have a message for Israel Spurlock,"

Immediately Captain Moseley knew that the placid and kindly face of Uncle Billy Powers had led him into making a mistake. He knew that he had mentioned Israel Spurlock's name to the wrong man at the wrong time. There was a scarcely perceptible frown on Uncle Billy's face as he raised it from his piece of pine bark, which was now assuming the shape of a horseman's pistol, and he looked at the captain through half-closed eyelids.

"Come, now," he exclaimed, " ain't Israel Spurlock in the war? Did n't a posse ketch 'im down yander in Jasper an' take an' cornscrip' 'im into the army? Run it over in your mind now! Ain't Israel Spurlock crippled some'r's, an' ain't your message for his poor ole mammy?"

"No, no," said the captain, laughing, and trying to hide his inward irritation.

"Not so?" exclaimed Uncle Billy. "Well, sir, you must be shore an' set me right when I go wrong; but I 'll tell you right pine blank, I 've had Israel Spurlock in my min' off an' on' ev'ry since they run him down an' kotch him an' drug 'im off to war. He was weakly like from the time he was a boy, an' when I heard you call forth his name, I allowed to myself, says I, 'Israel Spurlock is sick, an' they 've come atter his ole mammy to go an' nuss him.' That's the idee that riz up in my min'."

A man more shrewd than Captain Moseley would have been deceived by the bland simplicity of Uncle Billy's tone.

"No," said he; "Spurlock is not sick. He is a sounder man than I am. He was conscripted in Jasper and carried to Adairsville, and after he got used to the camp he concluded that he would come home and tell his folks good-by."

"Now that's jes like Israel," said Uncle Billy, closing his eyes and compressing his lips — "jes like him for the world. He knowed that he was drug off right spang at the time he wanted to be getherin' in his craps, an' savin' his ruffage, an' one thing an' another bekaze his ole mammy did n't have a soul to help her but 'im. I reckon he's been a-housin' his corn an' sich like. The ole 'oman tuck on might'ly when Israel was snatched into the army."

"How far is it to shelter?" inquired Captain Moseley.

"Not so mighty fur," responded Uncle Billy, whittling the pine bark more cautiously. "Jes keep in the middle of the road an' you'll soon come to it. Ef I ain't thar before you, jes holler for Aunt Crissy an' tell her that you saw Uncle Billy some'r's in the woods an' he told you to wait for 'im."

With that, Captain Moseley and Private Chadwick spurred their horses up the mountain road, leaving Uncle Billy whittling.

"Well, dang my buttons!" exclaimed Chadwick, when they were out of hearing.

"What now?" asked the captain, turning in his saddle. Private Chadwick had stopped his horse and was looking back down the mountain as if he expected to be pursued.

"I wish I may die," he went on, giving his horse the rein, "if we ain't walked right square into it with our eyes wide open."

"Into what?" asked the captain, curtly.

"Into trouble," said Chadwick. "Oh," he exclaimed, looking at his companion seriously, "you may grin behind your beard, but you just wait till the fun begins — all the grins you can muster will be mighty dry grins. Why, Cap., I could read that old chap as if he was a newspaper. Whilst he was a-watchin' you I was a-watchin' him, an' if he ain't got a war map printed on his face I ain't never saw none in the 'Charleston Mercury.'"

"The old man is a preacher," said Captain Moseley in a tone that seemed to dispose of the matter.

"Well, the Lord help us!" exclaimed Chadwick. "In about the wuss whippin' I ever got was from a young feller that was preachin' an' courtin' in my neighborhood. I sorter sassed him about a gal he was flyin' around, an' he upped an' frailed me out, an' got the gal to boot. Don't tell me about no preachers. Why, that chap flew at me like a Stonefence rooster, an' he fluttered twice to my once."

"And have you been running from preachers ever since?" dryly inquired the captain.

"Not as you may say, constantly a-runnin'," replied Chadwick; "yit I ain't been a-flingin' no sass at 'em; an' my reason tells me for to give 'em the whole wedth of the big road when I meet 'em."

"Well," said the captain, "what will you do about this preacher?"

"A man in a corner," responded Chadwick, "is obleeged to do the best he kin. I'll jest keep my eye on him, an' the fust motion he makes, I'll"—

"Run?" suggested the captain.

"Well, now," said Chadwick, "a man in a corner can't most ingener'lly run. Git me hemmed in, an' I'll scratch an' bite an' scuffle the best way I know how. It's human natur', an' I'm mighty glad it is; for if that old man's eyes did n't tell no lies we'll have to scratch an' scuffle before we git away from this mountain."

Captain Moseley bit his mustache and smiled grimly as the tired horses toiled up the road. A vague idea of possible danger had crossed his mind while talking to Uncle Billy Powers, but he dismissed it at once as a matter of little importance to a soldier bent on carrying out his orders at all hazards.

It was not long before the two travelers found themselves on a plateau formed by a shoulder of the mountain. On this plateau were abundant signs of life. Cattle were grazing about among the trees, chickens were crowing, and in the distance could be heard the sound of a woman's voice singing. As they pressed forward along the level road they came in sight of a cabin, and the blue smoke curling from its short chimney was suggestive of hospitality. It was a comfortable-looking cabin, too, flanked by several outhouses. The buildings, in contrast with the majestic bulk of the mountain, that still rose precipitously skyward, were curiously small, but there was an air of more than ordinary neatness and coziness about them. And there were touches of feminine hands here and there that made an impression — rows of well-kept boxwood winding like a green serpent through the yard, and a privet hedge that gave promise of rare sweetness in the spring.

As the soldiers approached, a dog barked, and then the singing ceased, and the figure of a young girl appeared in the doorway, only to disappear like a flash. This vision, vanishing with incredible swiftness, was succeeded by a more substantial one in the shape of a motherly looking woman, who stood gazing over her spectacles at the horsemen, apparently undecided whether to frown or to smile. The smile would have undoubtedly forced its way to the pleasant face in any event, for the years had fashioned many a pathway for it, but just then Uncle Billy Powers himself pushed the woman aside and made his appearance, laughing.

"'Light, boys, 'light!'" he exclaimed, walking nimbly to the gate. "'Light whilst

I off wi' your creeturs' gear. Ah!" he went on, as he busied himself unsaddling the horses, "you thought that while your Uncle Billy was a-moonin' aroun' down the hill yander you'd steal a march on your Aunt Crissy, an' maybe come a-conscriptin' of her into the army. But not — not so! Your Uncle Billy has been here long enough to get his hands an' his face rested."

"You must have been in a tremendous hurry," said Captain Moseley, remembering the weary length of mountain road he had climbed.

"Why, I could 'a' tuck a nap an' 'a' beat you," said the old man.

"Two miles of tough road, I should say," responded Moseley.

"Go straight through my hoss lot and let yourself down by a saplin' or two," answered Uncle Billy, "an' it ain't more 'n a good quarter." Whereupon the old man laughed heartily.

"Jes leave the creeturs here," he went on. "John Jeems an' Fillmore will ten' to 'em whilst we go in an' see what your Aunt Crissy is gwine to give us for supper. You won't find the grub so mighty various, but there is plenty enough of what they is."

There was just enough of deference in Aunt Crissy's greeting to be pleasing, and her unfeigned manifestations of hospitality soon caused the guests to forget that they might possibly be regarded as intruders in that peaceful region. Then there were the two boys, John Jeems and Fillmore, both large enough, and old enough, as Captain Moseley quietly observed to himself, to do military service, and both shy and awkward to a degree. And then there was Polly, a young woman grown, whose smiles all ran to blushes and dimples. Though she was grown, she had the ways of a girl — the vivacity of health and good humor, and the innocent shyness of a child of nature. Impulsive and demure by turns, her moods were whimsical and elusive and altogether delightful. Her beauty, which illumined the old cabin, was heightened by a certain quality that may be described as individuality. Her face and hands were browned by the sun, but in her cheeks the roses of youth and health played constantly. There is nothing more charming to the eye of man than the effects produced when modesty parts company with mere formality and conventionality. Polly, who was as shy as a ground squirrel and as graceful, never pestered herself about formalities. Innocence is not infrequently a very delightful form of boldness. It was so in the case of Polly Powers, at any rate.

The two rough soldiers, unused to the society of women, were far more awkward and constrained than the young woman, but they enjoyed the big fire and the comfortable supper none the less on that account. When, to employ Mrs. Powers's vernacular, " the things were put away," they brought forth their pipes; and they felt so contented that Captain Moseley reproved himself by suggesting that it might be well for them to proceed on their journey up the mountain. But their hosts refused to listen to such a proposal.

"Not so," exclaimed Uncle Billy; "by no means. Why, if you knowed this hill like we all, you 'd hoot at the bar' idee of gwine further after nightfall. Besides," the old man went on, looking keenly at his daughter, " ten to one you won't find Spurlock."

Polly had been playing with her hair, which was caught in a single plait and tied with a bit of scarlet ribbon. When Spurlock's name was mentioned she used the plait as a whip, and struck herself impatiently in the hand with the glossy black thong, and then threw it behind her, where it hung dangling nearly to the floor.

"Now I tell you what, boys," said Uncle Billy, after a little pause; "I'd jes like to know who is at the bottom of this Spurlock business. You all may have took a notion that he's a no-'count sorter chap — an' he is kinder puny; but what does the army want with a puny man?"

"It's the law," said Captain Moseley, simply, perceiving that his mission was clearly understood. "He is old enough and strong enough to serve in the army. The law calls for him, and he'll have to go. The law wants him now worse than ever."

"Yes," said private Chadwick, gazing into the glowing embers — "lots worse 'n ever."

"What's the matter along of him now?" inquired Mrs. Powers, knocking the ashes from her pipe against the chimney jamb.

"He's a deserter," said Chadwick.

"Tooby shore!" exclaimed Mrs. Powers. "An' what do they do wi' 'em, then?"

For answer Private Chadwick passed his

right hand rapidly around his neck, caught hold of an imaginary rope, and looked upwards at the rafters, rolling his eyes and distorting his features as though he were strangling. It was a very effective pantomime. Uncle Billy shook his head and groaned, Aunt Crissy lifted her hands in horror, and then both looked at Polly. That young lady had risen from her chair and made a step toward Chadwick. Her eyes were blazing.

"You'll be hung long before Israel Spurlock!" she cried, her voice thick with anger. Before another word had been said she swept from the room, leaving Chadwick sitting there with his mouth wide open.

"Don't let Polly pester you," said Uncle Billy, smiling a little at Chadwick's discomfiture. "She thinks the world an' all of Sister Spurlock, an' she's been a-knowin' Israel a mighty long time."

"Yes," said Aunt Crissy, with a sigh; "the poor child is hot-headed an' high-tempered. I reckon we've sp'ilt 'er. 'T ain't hard to spile a gal when you hain't got but one."

Before Chadwick could make reply a shrill, querulous voice was heard coming from the room into which Polly had gone. The girl had evidently aroused some one who was more than anxious to engage in a war of words.

"Lord A'mighty massy! whar's any peace?" the shrill voice exclaimed. "What chance on the top side of the yeth is a poor sick creetur got? Oh, what makes you come a-tromplin' on the floor like a drove of wild hosses, an' a-shakin' the clabberds on the roof? I know! I know!" — the voice here almost rose to a shriek, — "it's 'cause I'm sick an' weak, an' can't he'p myself. Lord! ef I but had strength!"

At this point Polly's voice broke in, but what she said could only be guessed by the noise in the next room.

"Well, what ef the house an' yard was full of 'em? Who's afeard? After Spurlock? Who keers? Hain't Spurlock got no friends on Sugar Mountain? Ef they are after Spurlock, ain't Spurlock got as good a right for to be after them? Oh, go 'way! Gals hain't got no sense. Go 'way! Go tell your pappy to come here an' he'p me in my cheer. Oh, go on!"

Polly had no need to go, however. Uncle Billy rose promptly and went into the next room.

"Hit's daddy," said Aunt Crissy, by way of explanation. "Lord! daddy used to be a mighty man in his young days, but he's that wasted wi' the palsy that he hain't more 'n a shadder of what he was. He's jes like a baby, an' he's mighty quar'lsome when the win' sets in from the east."

According to all symptoms the wind was at that moment setting terribly from the east. There was a sound of shuffling in the next room, and then Uncle Billy Powers came into the room, bearing in his stalwart arms a big rocking-chair containing a little old man whose body and limbs were shriveled and shrunken. Only his head, which seemed to be abnormally large, had escaped the ravages of whatever disease had seized him. His eyes were bright as a bird's and his forehead was noble in its proportions.

"Gentlemen," said Uncle Billy, "this here is Colonel Dick Watson. He used to be a big politicianer in his day an' time. He's my father-in-law."

Uncle Billy seemed to be wonderfully proud of his connection with Colonel Watson. As for the Colonel, he eyed the strangers closely, apparently forgetting to respond to their salutation.

"I reckon you think it's mighty fine, thish 'ere business er gwine ter war whar they hain't nobody but peaceable folks," exclaimed the colonel, his shrill, metallic voice being in curious contrast to his emaciated figure.

"Daddy!" said Mrs. Powers in a warning tone.

"Lord A'mighty! don't pester me, Crissy Jane. Hain't I done seed war before? When I was in the legislatur' did n't the boys rig up an' march away to Mexico? But you know yourself," the colonel went on, turning to Uncle Billy's guests, "that this hain't Mexico, an' that they hain't no war gwine on on this 'ere hill. You know that mighty well."

"But there's a tolerable big one going on over yonder," said Captain Moseley, with a sweep of his hand to the westward.

"Now, you don't say!" exclaimed Colonel Watson, sarcastically. "A big war going on an' you all quiled up here before the fire, out 'n sight an' out 'n hearin'! Well, well, well!"

"We are here on business," said Captain Moseley, gently.

"Tooby shore!" said the Colonel, with a

sinister screch that was intended to simulate laughter. "You took the words out 'n my mouth. I was in-about ready to say it when you upped an' said it yourself. War gwine on over yander an' you all up here on business. Crissy Jane," remarked the colonel in a different tone, "come here an' wipe my face an' see ef I 'm a-sweatin'. Ef I 'm a-sweatin', hit 's the fust time since Sadday before last."

Mrs. Powers mopped her father's face, and assured him that she felt symptoms of perspiration.

"Oh, yes!" continued the colonel. "Business here an' war yander. I hear tell that you er after Israel Spurlock. Lord A'mighty above us! What er you after Israel for? He hain't got no niggers for to fight for. All the fightin' he can do is to fight for his ole mammy."

Captain Moseley endeavored to explain to Colonel Watson why his duty made it imperatively necessary to carry Spurlock back to the conscript camp, but in the midst of it all the old man cried out: —

"Oh, I know who sent you!"

"Who?" the captain said.

"Nobody but Wesley Lovejoy!"

Captain Moseley made no response, but gazed into the fire. Chadwick, on the other hand, when Lovejoy's name was mentioned, slapped himself on the leg, and straightened himself up with the air of a man who has made an interesting discovery.

"Come, now," Colonel Watson insisted, "hain't it so? Did n't Wesley Lovejoy send you?"

"Well," said Moseley, "a man named Lovejoy is on Colonel Waring's staff, and he gave me my orders."

At this the old man fairly shrieked with laughter, and so sinister was its emphasis that the two soldiers felt the cold chills creeping up their backs.

"What is the matter with Lovejoy?" It was Chadwick who spoke.

"Oh, wait!" cried Colonel Watson; "thes wait. You may n't want to wait, but you'll have to. I may look like I'm mighty puny, an' I 'spec' I am, but I hain't dead yit. Lord A'mighty, no! Not by a long shot!"

There was a pause here, during which Aunt Crissy remarked, in a helpless sort of way: —

"I wonder wher' Polly is, an' what she's a-doin'?"

"Don't pester 'long of Polly," snapped the paralytic. "She knows what she's a-doin'."

"About this Wesley Lovejoy," said Captain Moseley, turning to the old man: "you seem to know him very well."

"You hear that, William!" exclaimed Colonel Watson. "He asts me ef I know Wes. Lovejoy! Do I know him? Why, the triflin' houn'! I've knowed him ev'ry sence he was big enough to rob a hen-roos'."

Uncle Billy Powers, in his genial way, tried to change the current of conversation, and he finally succeeded, but it was evident that Adjutant Lovejoy had one enemy, if not several, in that humble household. Such was the feeling for Spurlock and contempt for Wesley Lovejoy that Captain Moseley and Private Chadwick felt themselves to be interlopers, and they once more suggested the necessity of pursuing their journey. This suggestion seemed to amuse the paralytic, who laughed loudly.

"Lord A'mighty!" he exclaimed, "I know how you feel, an' I don't blame you for feelin' so; but don't you go up the mountain this night. Thes stay right whar you is, beca'se ef you don't you'll make all your friends feel bad for you. Don't ast me how, don't ast me why. Thes you stay. Come an' put me to bed, William, an' don't let these folks go out 'n the house this night."

Uncle Billy carried the old man into the next room, tucked him away in his bed, and then came back. Conversation lagged to such an extent that Aunt Crissy once more felt moved to inquire about Polly. Uncle Billy responded with a sweeping gesture of his right hand, which might mean much or little. To the two Confederates it meant nothing, but to Aunt Crissy it said that Polly had gone up the mountain in the rain and cold. Involuntarily the woman shuddered and drew nearer the fire.

It was in fact a venturesome journey that Polly had undertaken. Hardened as she was to the weather, familiar as she was with the footpaths that led up and down and around the face of the mountain, her heart rose in her mouth when she found herself fairly on the way to Israel Spurlock's house. The darkness was almost overwhelming in its intensity. As Uncle Billy Powers remarked while showing the two Confederates to their beds in the "shed-room," there " was a solid chunk of it from one eend of creation to t' other." The rain, falling steadily but not heavily, was bitterly cold, and it was made more uncomfortable by the wind, which rose and fell with a muffled roar, like the sigh of some Titanic spirit flying hither and yonder in the wild recesses of the sky. Bold as she was, the girl was appalled by the invisible contention that seemed to be going on in the elements above her, and more than once she paused, ready to flee, as best she could, back to the light and warmth she had left behind; but the gesture of Chadwick, with its cruel significance, would recur to her, and then, clenching her teeth, she would press blindly on. She was carrying a message of life and freedom to Israel Spurlock.

With the rain dripping from her hair and her skirts, her face and hands benumbed with cold, but with every nerve strung to the highest tension and every faculty alert to meet whatever danger might present itself, Polly struggled up the mountain path, feeling her way as best she could, and pulling herself along by the aid of the friendly saplings and the overhanging trees.

After a while — and it seemed a long while to Polly, contending with the fierce forces of the night and beset by a thousand doubts and fears — she could hear Spurlock's dogs barking. What if the two soldiers, suspecting her mission, had mounted their horses and outstripped her? She had no time to remember the difficulties of the mountain road, nor did she know that she had been on her journey not more than half an hour. She was too excited either to reason or to calculate. Gathering her skirts in her hands as she rose to the level of the clearing, Polly rushed across it towards the little cabin, tore open the frail little gate, and flung herself against the door with a force that shook the house.

Old Mrs. Spurlock was spinning, while Israel carded the rolls for her. The noise that Polly made against the door startled them both. The thread broke in Mrs. Spurlock's hand, and one part of it curled itself on the end of the broach with a buzz that whirled it into a fantastically tangled mass. The cards dropped from Israel's hands with a clatter that added to his mother's excitement.

"Did anybody ever hear the beat of that?" she exclaimed. "Run, Iserl, an' see what it is that's a-tryin' to tear the roof off 'n the house."

Israel did not need to be told, nor did Mrs. Spurlock wait for him to go. They reached the door together, and when Israel threw it open they saw Polly Powers standing there, pale, trembling, and dripping.

"Polly!" cried Israel, taking her by the arm. He could say no more.

"In the name er the Lord!" exclaimed Mrs. Spurlock, "wher' 'd you drop from? You look more like a drownded ghost than you does like folks. Come right in here an' dry yourse'f. What in the name of mercy brung you out in sech weather? Who's dead or a-dyin'? Why, look at the gal!" Mrs. Spurlock went on in a louder tone, seeing that Polly stood staring at them with wide-open eyes, her face as pale as death.

"Have they come?" gasped Polly.

"Listen at 'er, Iserl! I b'lieve in my soul she's done gone an' run ravin' deestracted. Shake 'er, Iserl; shake 'er."

For answer Polly dropped forward into Mrs. Spurlock's arms, all wet as she was, and there fell to crying in a way that was quite alarming to Israel, who was not familiar with feminine peculiarities. Mrs. Spurlock soothed Polly as she would have soothed a baby, and half carried, half led her to the fireplace. Israel, who was standing around embarrassed and perplexed, was driven out of the room, and soon Polly was decked out in dry clothes. These "duds," as Mrs. Spurlock called them, were ill-fitting and ungraceful, but in Israel's eyes the girl was just as beautiful as ever. She was even more beautiful when, fully recovered from her excitement, she told with sparkling eyes and heightened color the story she had to tell.

Mrs. Spurlock listened with the keenest interest, and with many an exclamation of indignation, while Israel heard it with undisguised admiration for the girl. He seemed to enjoy the whole proceeding, and when Polly in the ardor and excitement of her narration betrayed an almost passionate interest in his probable fate, he rubbed his hands slowly together and laughed softly to himself.

"An' jest to think," exclaimed Polly, when she had finished her story, "that that there good-for-nothin' Wesley Lovejoy had the imperdence to ast me to have him no longer 'n last year, an' he's been a-flyin' round me constant."

"I seed him a-droppin' his wing," said

Israel, laughing. "I reckon that's the reason he's after me so hot. But never you mind, mammy; you thes look after the gal that's gwine to be your daughter-in-law, an' I'll look after your son."

"Go off, you goose!" cried Polly, blushing and smiling. "Ef they hang you, whose daughter-in-law will I be then?"

"The Lord knows!" exclaimed Israel, with mock seriousness. "They tell me that Lovejoy is an orphan!"

"You must be crazy," cried Polly, indignantly. "I hope you don't think I'd marry that creetur. I wouldn't look at him if he was the last man. You better be thinkin' about your goozle."

"It's ketchin' befo' hangin'," said Israel,

"They've mighty nigh got you now," said Polly. Just then a hickory nut dropped on the roof of the house, and the noise caused the girl to start up with an exclamation of terror.

"You thought they had me then," said Israel, as he rose and stood before the fire, rubbing his hands together, and seeming to enjoy most keenly the warm interest the girl manifested in his welfare.

"Oh, I wisht you'd cut an' run," pleaded

Polly, covering her face with her hands; "they 'll be here therreckly."

Israel was not a bad-looking fellow as he stood before the fire laughing. He was a very agreeable variation of the mountain type. He was angular, but neither stoop-shouldered nor cadaverous. He was awkward in his manners, but very gracefully fashioned. In point of fact, as Mrs. Powers often remarked, Israel was "not to be sneezed at."

After a while he became thoughtful. "I jest tell you what," he said, kicking the chunks vigorously, and sending little sparks of fire skipping and cracking about the room. "This business puzzles me — I jest tell you it does. That Wes. Lovejoy done like he was the best friend I had. He was constantly huntin' me up in camp, an' when I told him I would like to come home an' git mammy's crap in, he jest laughed an' said he did n't reckon I 'd be missed much, an' now he 's a-houndin' me down. What has the man got agin me?"

Polly knew, but she did n't say. Mrs. Spurlock suspected, but she made no effort to enlighten Israel. Polly knew that Lovejoy was animated by blind jealousy, and her instinct taught her that a jealous man is usually a dangerous one. Taking advantage of one of the privileges of her sex, she had at one time carried on a tremendous flirtation with Lovejoy. She had intended to amuse herself simply, but she had kindled fires she was powerless to quench. Lovejoy had taken her seriously, and she knew well enough that he regarded Israel Spurlock as a rival. She had reason to suspect, too, that Lovejoy had pointed out Israel to the conscript officers, and that the same influence was controlling and directing the pursuit now going on.

Under the circumstances, her concern — her alarm, indeed — was natural. She and Israel had been sweethearts for years, — real sure-enough sweethearts, as she expressed it to her grandfather, — and they were to be married in a short while; just as soon, in fact, as the necessary preliminaries of clothes-making and cake-baking could be disposed of. She thought nothing of her feat of climbing the mountain in the bitter cold and the overwhelming rain. She would have taken much larger risks than that; she would have faced any danger her mind could conceive of. And Israel appreciated it all; nay, he fairly gloated over it. He stood before the fire fairly hugging the fact to his bosom. His face glowed, and his whole attitude was one of exultation; and with it, shaping every gesture and movement, was a manifestation of fearlessness which was all the more impressive because it was unconscious.

This had a tendency to fret Polly, whose alarm for Israel's safety was genuine.

"Oh, I do wisht you 'd go on," she cried; "them men 'll shorely ketch you ef you keep on a-stayin' here a-winkin' an' a-gwine on makin' monkey motions."

"Shoo!" exclaimed Israel. "Ef the house was surrounded by forty thousan' of 'em, I 'd git by 'em, an', ef need be, take you wi' me."

While they were talking the dogs began to bark. At the first sound Polly rose from her chair with her arms outstretched, but fell back pale and trembling. Israel had disappeared as if by magic, and Mrs. Spurlock was calmly lighting her pipe by filling it with hot embers. It was evidently a false alarm, for, after a while, Israel backed through the doorway and closed the door again with comical alacrity.

"Sh-sh-sh!" he whispered, with a warning gesture, seeing that Polly was about to protest. "Don't make no fuss. The dogs has been a-barkin' at sperits an' things. Jest keep right still."

He went noiselessly about the room, picking up first one thing and then another. Over one shoulder he flung a canteen, and over the other a hunting-horn. Into his coat-pocket he thrust an old-fashioned powder-flask. Meanwhile his mother was busy gathering together such articles as Israel might need. His rifle she placed by the door, and then she filled a large homespun satchel with a supply of victuals — a baked fowl, a piece of smoked beef, and a big piece of light bread. These preparations were swiftly and silently made. When everything seemed to be ready for his departure Israel presented the appearance of a peddler.

"I'm goin' up to the Rock," he said, by way of explanation, "an' light the fire. Maybe the boys 'll see it, an' maybe they won't. Leastways they're mighty apt to smell the smoke."

Then, without further farewell, he closed the door and stepped out into the darkness, leaving the two women sitting by the hearth. They sat there for hours, gazing into the fire and scarcely speaking to each other. The curious reticence that seems to be developed and assiduously cultivated by the dwellers on the mountains took possession of them. The confidences and sympathies they had in common were those of observation and experience, rather than the result of an interchange of views and opinions.

Towards morning the drizzling rain ceased, and the wind, changing its direction, sent the clouds flying to the east, whence they had come. About dawn, Private Chadwick, who had slept most soundly, was aroused by the barking of the dogs, and got up to look after the horses. As he slipped quietly out of the house he saw a muffled figure crossing the yard.

"Halt!" he cried, giving the challenge of a sentinel. "Who goes there?"

"Nobody ner nothin' that 'll bite you, I reckon," was the somewhat snappish response. It was the voice of Polly. She was looking up and across the mountains to where a bright red glare was reflected on the scurrying clouds. The density of the atmosphere was such that the movements of the flames were photographed on the clouds, rising and falling, flaring and fading, as though the dread spirits of the storm were waving their terrible red banners from the mountain.

"What can that be?" asked Chadwick, after he had watched the singular spectacle a moment.

Polly laughed aloud, almost joyously. She knew it was Israel's beacon. She knew that these red reflections, waving over the farther spur of the mountain and over the valley that nestled so peacefully below, would summon half a hundred men and boys — the entire congregation of Antioch Church, where her father was in the habit of holding forth on the first Sunday of each month. She knew that Israel was safe, and the knowledge restored her good humor.

"What did you say it was?" Chadwick inquired again, his curiosity insisting on an explanation.

"It's jest a fire, I reckon," Polly calmly replied. "Ef it's a house burnin' down, it can't be holp. Water could n't save it now."

Whereupon she pulled the shawl from over her head, tripped into the house, and went about preparing breakfast, singing merrily. Chadwick watched her as she passed and repassed from the rickety kitchen to the house, and when the light grew clearer he thought he saw on her face a look that he did not understand. It was indeed an inscrutable expression, and it would have puzzled a wiser man than Chadwick. He chopped some wood, brought some water, and made himself generally useful; but he received no thanks from Polly. She ignored him as completely as if he had never existed.

All this set the private to thinking. Now a man who reflects much usually thinks out a theory to fit everything that he fails to understand. Chadwick thought out his theory while the girl was getting breakfast ready.

It was not long before the two soldiers were on their way up the mountain, nor was it long before Chadwick began to unfold his theory, and in doing so he managed to straighten it by putting together various little facts that occurred to him as he talked.

"I tell you what, Captain," he said, as soon as they were out of hearing; "that gal's a slick 'un. It's my belief that we are gwine on a fool's errand. 'Stead of gwine towards Spurlock, we 're gwine straight away from 'im. When that gal made her disappearance last night she went an' found Spurlock, an' ef he ain't a natchul born fool he tuck to the woods. Why, the shawl the gal had on her head this mornin' was soakin' wet. It were n't rainin', an' had n't been for a right smart while. How come the shawl wet? They were n't but one way. It got wet by rubbin' agin the bushes an' the limbs er the trees."

This theory was plausible enough to impress itself on Captain Moseley. "What is to be done, then?" he asked.

"Well, the Lord knows what ought to be done," said Chadwick; "but I reckon the best plan is to sorter scatter out an' skirmish aroun' a little bit. We 'd better divide our army. You go up the mountain an' git Spurlock, if he 's up thar, an' let me take my stan' on the ridge yander an' keep my eye on Uncle Billy's back yard an' hoss lot. If Spurlock is r'ally tuck to the woods, he 'll be mighty apt to be slinkin' 'roun' whar the gal is."

Captain Moseley assented to this plan, and proceeded to put it in execution as soon as he and Chadwick were a safe distance from Uncle Billy Powers's house. Chadwick, dismounting, led his horse along a cowpath that ran at right angles to the main road, and was soon lost to sight, while the captain rode forward on his mission.

Of the two, as it turned out, the captain had much the more comfortable experience. He reached the Spurlock house in the course of three-quarters of an hour.

In response to his halloo Mrs. Spurlock came to the door.

"I was a-spinnin' away for dear life," she remarked, brushing her gray hair from her face, "when all of a sudden I hearn a fuss, an' I 'lows ter myself, says I, 'I 'll be boun' that 's some one a-hailin',' says I; an' then I dropped ever'thin' an' run ter the door an' shore enough it was. Won't you 'light an' come in?" she inquired with ready hospitality. Her tone was polite, almost obsequious.

"Is Mr. Israel Spurlock at home?" the captain asked.

"Not, as you might say, adzackly at home, but I reckon in reason it won't be long before he draps in. He hain't had his breakfas' yit, though hit 's been a-waitin' for him tell hit 's stone col'. The cows broke out last night, an' he went off a-huntin' of 'em time it was light good. Iserl is thes ez rank after his milk ez some folks is after the'r dram. I says, says I, 'Shorely you kin do 'thout your milk one mornin' in the year;' but he wouldn't nigh hear ter that. He thes up an' bolted off."

"I'll ride on," said the captain. "Maybe I'll meet him coming back. Good-by."

It was an uneventful ride, but Captain Moseley noted one curious fact. He had not proceeded far when he met two men riding down the mountain. Each carried a rifle flung across his saddle in front of him. They responded gravely to the captain's salutation.

"Have you seen Israel Spurlock this morning?" he asked.

"No, sir, I hain't saw him," answered one. The other shook his head. Then they rode on down the mountain.

A little farther on Captain Moseley met four men. These were walking, but each was armed — three with rifles, and one with a shot-gun. They had not seen Spurlock. At intervals he met more than a dozen — some riding and some walking, but all armed. At last he met two that presented something of a contrast to the others. They were armed, it is true; but they were laughing and singing as they went along the road, and while they had not seen Spurlock with their own eyes, as they said, they knew he must be farther up the mountain, for they had heard of him as they came along.

Riding and winding around upward, Captain Moseley presently saw a queer-looking little chap coming towards him. The little man had a gray beard, and as he walked he had a movement like a camel. Like a camel, too, he had a great hump on his back. His legs were as long as any man's, but his whole body seemed to be contracted in his hump. He was very spry, too, moving along as active as a boy, and there was an elfish expression on his face such as one sees in old picture-books — a cunning, leering expression, which yet had for its basis the element of humor. The little man carried a rifle longer than himself, which he flourished about with surprising ease and dexterity — practicing apparently some new and peculiar manual.

"Have you seen Israel Spurlock?" inquired Captain Moseley, reining in his horse.

"Yes! Oh, yes! Goodness gracious, yes!" replied the little man, grinning good-naturedly.

"Where is he now?" asked the captain.

"All about. Yes! All around! Gracious, yes!" responded the little man, with a sweeping gesture that took in the whole mountain. Then he seemed to be searching eagerly in the road for something. Suddenly pausing, he exclaimed: "Here's his track right now! Oh, yes! Right fresh, too! Goodness, yes!"

"Where are you going?" Moseley asked, smiling at the antics of the little man, their nimbleness being out of all proportion to his deformity.

For answer the little man whirled his rifle over his hump and under his arm, and caught it as it went flying into the air. Then he held it at a "ready," imitating the noise of the lock with his mouth, took aim and made believe to fire, all with indescribable swiftness and precision. Captain Moseley rode on his way laughing; but, laugh as he would, he could not put out of his mind the queer impression the little man had made on him, nor could he rid himself of a feeling of uneasiness. Taking little notice of the landmarks that ordinarily attract the notice of the traveler in a strange country, he suddenly found himself riding along a level stretch of tableland. The transformation was complete. The country roads seemed to cross and recross here, coming and going in every direction. He rode by a little house that stood alone in the level wood, and he rightly judged it to be a church. He drew rein and looked around him. Everything was unfamiliar. In the direction from which he supposed he had come, a precipice rose sheer from the tableland more than three hundred feet. At that moment he heard a shout, and looking up he beheld the hunchback flourishing his long rifle and cutting his queer capers.

The situation was so puzzling that Captain Moseley passed his hand over his eyes, as if to brush away a scene that confused his mind and obstructed his vision. He turned his horse and rode back the way he had come, but it seemed to be so unfamiliar that he chose another road, and in the course of a quarter of an hour he was compelled to acknowledge that he was lost. Everything appeared to be turned around, even the little church.

Meanwhile Private Chadwick was having an experience of his own. In parting from Captain Moseley he led his horse through the bushes, following for some distance a cow-path. This semblance of a trail terminated in a "blind path," and this Chadwick followed as best he could, picking his way cautiously and choosing ground over which his horse could follow. He had to be very careful. There were no leaves on the trees, and the undergrowth was hardly thick enough to conceal him from the keen eyes of the mountaineers. Finally he tied his horse in a thicket of black-jacks, where he had the whole of Uncle Billy Powers's little farm under his eye. His position was not an uncomfortable one. Sheltered from the wind, he had nothing to do but sit on a huge chestnut log and ruminate, and make a note of the comings and goings on Uncle Billy's premises.

Sitting thus, Chadwick fell to thinking; thinking, he fell into a doze. He caught himself nodding more than once, and upbraided himself bitterly. Still he nodded — he, a soldier on duty at his post. How long he slept he could not tell, but he suddenly awoke to find himself dragged backward from the log by strong hands. He would have made some resistance, for he was a fearless man at heart and a tough one to handle in a knock-down and drag-out tussle; but resistance was useless. He had been taken at a disadvantage, and before he could make a serious effort in his own behalf, he was lying flat on his back, with his hands tied, and as helpless as an infant. He looked up and discovered that his captor was Israel Spurlock.

"Well, blame my scaly hide!" exclaimed Chadwick, making an involuntary effort to free his hands. "You're the identical man I'm a-huntin'."

"An' now you're sorry you went an' foun' me, I reckon," said Israel.

"Well, I ain't as glad as I 'lowed I'd be," said Chadwick. "Yit nuther am I so mighty sorry. One way or 'nother I knowed in reason I'd run up on you."

"You're mighty right," responded Israel, smiling not ill-naturedly. "You fell in my arms same as a gal in a honeymoon. Lemme lift you up, as the mule said when he kicked the nigger over the fence. Maybe you'll look purtier when you swap een's." Thereupon Israel helped Chadwick to his feet.

"You ketched me that time, certain and shore," said the latter, looking at Spurlock and laughing; "they ain't no two ways about that. I was a-settin' on the log thar, a-noddin' an' a-dreamin' 'bout Christmas. 'T ain't many days off, I reckon."

"Oh, yes!" exclaimed Spurlock, sarcastically; "a mighty purty dream, I bet a hoss. You was fixin' up for to cram me in Lovejoy's stockin'. A mighty nice present I 'd 'a' been, tooby shore. Stidder hangin' up his stockin', Lovejoy was a-aimin' for to hang me up. Oh, yes! Christmas dreams is so mighty nice an' fine, I 'm a great min' to set right down here an' have one er my own — one of them kin' er dreams what 's got forked tail an' fireworks mixed up on it."

"Well," said Chadwick, with some seriousness, "whose stockin' is you a-gwine to cram me in?"

"In whose else's but Danny Lemmons's? An' won't he holler an' take on? Why, I would n't miss seein' Danny Lemmons take on for a hat full er shinplasters. Dang my buttons ef I would!"

Chadwick looked at his captor with some curiosity. There was not a trace of ill-feeling or bad humor in Spurlock's tone, nor in his attitude. The situation was so queer that it was comical, and Chadwick laughed aloud as he thought about it. In this Spurlock heartily joined him, and the situation would have seemed doubly queer to a passer-by chancing along and observing captor and prisoner laughing and chatting so amiably together.

"Who, in the name of goodness, is Danny Lemmons?"

"Lord!" exclaimed Spurlock, lifting both hands, "don't ast me about Danny Lemmons. He 's — he 's — well, I tell you what, he 's the bull er the woods, Danny Lemmons is; nuther more ner less. He hain't bigger 'n my two fists, an' he 's 'flicted, an' he 's all crippled up in his back, whar he had it broke when he was a baby, an' yit he 's in-about the peartest man on the mountain, an' he 's the toughest an' the sooplest. An' more 'n that, he 's got them things up here," Spurlock went on, tapping his head significantly. Chadwick understood this to mean that Lemmons, whatever might be his afflictions, had brains enough and to spare.

There was a pause in the conversation, and then Chadwick, looking at his bound wrists, which were beginning to chafe and swell, spoke up.

"What's your will wi' me?" he asked.

"Well," said Spurlock, rising to his feet, "I'm a-gwine to empty your gun, an' tote your pistol for you, an' invite you down to Uncle Billy's. Oh, you need n't worry," he went on, observing Chadwick's disturbed expression, "they're expectin' of you. Polly's tol' 'em you'd likely come back."

"How did Polly know?" Chadwick inquired.

"Danny Lemmons tol' 'er."

"By George!" exclaimed Chadwick, "the woods is full of Danny Lemmons."

"Why, bless your heart," said Spurlock, "he thes swarms roun' here."

After Spurlock had taken the precaution to possess himself of Chadwick's arms and ammunition, he cut the cords that bound his prisoner's hands, and the two went down the mountain, chatting as pleasantly and as sociably as two boon companions. Chadwick found no lack of hospitality at Uncle Billy Powers's house. His return was taken as a matter of course, and he was made welcome. Nevertheless, his entertainers betrayed a spirit of levity that might have irritated a person less self-contained.

"I see he's ketched you, Iserl," remarked Uncle Billy, with a twinkle in his eye. "He 'lowed las' night as how he'd fetch you back wi' him."

"Yes," said Israel, "he thes crope up on me. It's mighty hard for to fool these army fellers."

Then and afterward the whole family pretended to regard Spurlock as Chadwick's prisoner. This was not a joke for the latter to relish, but it was evidently not intended to be offensive, and he could do no less than humor it. He accepted the situation philosophically. He even prepared himself to relish Captain Moseley's astonishment when he returned and discovered the true state of affairs. As the day wore away it occurred to Chadwick that the captain was in no hurry to return. Even Uncle Billy Powers grew uneasy.

"Now, I do hope an' trust he ain't gone an' lost his temper up thar in the woods," remarked Uncle Billy. "I hope it from the bottom of my heart. These here wars an' rumors of wars makes the folks mighty restless. They'll take resks now what they wouldn't dassent to of tuck before this here rippit begun, an' it's done got so now human life ain't wuth shucks. The boys up here ain't no better 'n the rest. They fly to pieces quicker 'n they ever did."

No trouble, however, had come to Captain Moseley. Though he was confused in his bearings, he was as serene and as unruffled as when training a company of raw conscripts in the art of war. After an unsuccessful attempt to find the road he gave his horse the rein, and that sensible animal, his instinct sharpened by remembrance of Uncle Billy Powers's corn-crib and fodder, moved about at random until he found that he was really at liberty to go where he pleased, and then he turned short about, struck a little canter, and was soon going down the road by which he had come. The captain was as proud of this feat as if it were due to his own intelligence, and he patted the horse's neck in an approving way.

As Captain Moseley rode down the mountain, reflecting, it occurred to him that his expedition was taking a comical shape. He had gone marching up the hill, and now he came marching down again, and Israel Spurlock, so far as the captain knew, was as far from being a captive as ever — perhaps farther. Thinking it all over in a somewhat irritated frame of mind, Moseley remembered Lovejoy's eagerness to recapture Spurlock. He remembered, also, what he had heard the night before, and it was in no pleasant mood that he thought it all over. It was such an insignificant, such a despicable affair, two men carrying out the jealous whim of a little militia politician.

"It is enough, by George!" exclaimed Captain Moseley aloud, "to make a sensible man sick."

"Lord, yes!" cried out a voice behind him. Looking around, he saw the hunchback following him. "That's what I tell 'em; goodness, yes!"

"Now, look here!" said Captain Moseley, reining in his horse, and speaking somewhat sharply. "Are you following me, or am I following you? I don't want to be dogged after in the bushes, much less in the big road."

"Ner me nurther," said the hunchback, in the cheerfulest manner. "An' then thar's Spurlock — Lord, yes; I hain't axt him about it, but I bet a hoss he don't like to be dogged atter nuther."

"My friend," said Captain Moseley, "you

seem to have a quick tongue. What is your name?"

"Danny Lemmons," said the other. "Now don't say I look like I ought to be squoze. Ever'body inginer'lly says that," he went on with a grimace, "but I've squoze lots more than what's ever squoze me. Lord, yes! Yes, siree! Men an' gals tergether. You ax 'em, an' they'll tell you."

"Lemmons," said the captain, repeating the name slowly. "Well, you look it!"

"Boo!" cried Danny Lemmons, making a horrible grimace; "you don't know what you're a-talkin' about. The gals all 'low I'm mighty sweet. You ought to see me when I'm rigged out in my Sunday-go-to-meetin' duds. Polly Powers she 'lows I look snatchin'. Lord, yes! Yes, siree! I'm gwine down to Polly's house now."

Whereat he broke out singing, paraphrasing an old negro ditty, and capering about in the woods like mad.

> Oh, I went down to Polly's house,
>   An' she was not at home;
> I set myself in the big arm-cheer
>   An' beat on the ol' jaw-bone.
> Oh, rise up, Polly! Slap 'im on the jaw,
>   An hit 'im in the eyeball — bim!"

The song finished, Danny Lemmons

walked on down the road ahead of the horse in the most unconcerned manner. It was part of Captain Moseley's plan to stop at Mrs. Spurlock's and inquire for Israel. This seemed to be a part of Danny's plan also, for he turned out of the main road and went ahead, followed by the captain. There were quite a number of men at Mrs. Spurlock's when Moseley rode up, and he noticed that all were armed. Some were standing listlessly about, leaning against the trees, some were sitting in various postures, and others were squatting around whittling: but all had their guns within easy reach. Mrs. Spurlock was walking about among them smoking her pipe. By the strained and awkward manner of the men as they returned his salutation, or by some subtle instinct he could not explain, Captain Moseley knew that these men were waiting for him, and that he was their prisoner. The very atmosphere seemed to proclaim the fact. Under his very eyes Danny Lemmons changed from a grinning buffoon into a quiet, self-contained man trained to the habit of command. Recognizing the situation, the old soldier made the most of it by retaining his good humor.

"Well, boys," he said, flinging a leg over the pommel of his saddle, "I hope you are not tired waiting for me." The men exchanged glances in a curious, shame-faced sort of way.

"No," said one; "we was thes a-settin' here talkin' 'bout ol' times. We 'lowed maybe you 'd sorter git tangled up on the hill thar, and so Danny Lemmons, he harked back for to keep a' eye on you."

There was no disposition on the part of this quiet group of men to be clamorous or boastful. There was a certain shyness in their attitude, as of men willing to apologize for what might seem to be unnecessary rudeness.

"I 'll tell you what," said Danny Lemmons, "they ain't a man on the mounting that 's got a blessed thing agin you, ner agin the tother feller, an' they hain't a man anywheres aroun' here that 's a-gwine to pester you. We never brung you whar you is; but now that you 're here we 're a-gwine to whirl in an' ast you to stay over an' take Christmas wi' us, sech ez we 'll have. Lord, yes! a nice time we 'll have, ef I ain't forgot how to finger the fiddle-strings. We 're sorter in a quandary," Danny Lemmons continued, observing Captain Moseley toying nervously with the handle of his pistol. "We don't know whether you're a-gwine to be worried enough to start a row, or whether you're a-gwine to work up trouble."

Meanwhile Danny had brought his long rifle into a position where it could be used promptly and effectually. For answer Moseley dismounted from his horse, unbuckled his belt and flung it across his saddle, and prepared to light his pipe.

"Now, then," said Danny Lemmons, "thes make yourself at home."

Nothing could have been friendlier than the attitude of the mountain men, nor freer than their talk. Captain Moseley learned that Danny Lemmons was acting under the orders of Colonel Dick Watson, the virile paralytic; that he and Chadwick were to be held prisoners in the hope that Adjutant Lovejoy would come in search of them — in which event there would be developments of a most interesting character.

So Danny Lemmons said, and so it turned out; for one day while Moseley and Chadwick were sitting on the sunny side of Uncle Billy's house, listening to the shrill, snarling tones of Colonel Watson, they heard a shout from the roadside, and behold, there was Danny Lemmons with his little band escorting Lovejoy and a small squad of forlorn-looking militia. Lovejoy was securely bound to his horse, and it may well be supposed that he did not cut an imposing figure. Yet he was undaunted. He was captured, but not conquered. His eyes never lost their boldness, nor his tongue its bitterness. He was almost a match for Colonel Watson, who raved at all things through the tremulous and vindictive lips of disease. The colonel's temper was fitful, but Lovejoy's seemed to burn steadily. Moved by contempt rather than caution, he was economical of his words, listening to the shrill invective of the colonel patiently, but with a curious flicker of his thin lips that caused Danny Lemmons to study him intently. It was Danny who discovered that Lovejoy's eyes never wandered in Polly's direction, nor settled on her, nor seemed to perceive that she was in existence, though she was flitting about constantly on the aimless little errands that keep a conscientious housekeeper busy.

Lovejoy was captured one morning and

Christmas fell the next, and it was a memorable Christmas to all concerned. After breakfast Uncle Billy Powers produced his Bible and preached a little sermon — a sermon that was not the less meaty and sincere, not the less wise and powerful, because the English was ungrammatical and the rhetoric uncouth. After it was over the old man cleared his throat and remarked: —

"Brethern, we're gethered here for to praise the Lord an' do his will. The quare times that's come on us has brung us face to face with much that is unseemly in life, an' likely to fret the sperit an' vex the understandin'. Yit the Almighty is with us, an' of us, an' among us; an', in accordance wi' the commands delivered in this Book, we're here to fortify two souls in the'r choice, an' to b'ar testimony to the Word that makes lawful marriage a sacrament."

With that, Uncle Billy, fumbling in his coat pockets, produced a marriage license, called Israel Spurlock and his daughter before him, and in simple fashion pronounced the words that made them man and wife.

The dinner that followed hard on the wedding was to the soldiers, who had been subsisting on the tough rations furnished by the

Confederate commissaries, by all odds the chief event of the day. To them the resources of the Powers household were wonderful indeed. The shed-room, running the whole length of the house and kitchen, was utilized, and the dinner table, which was much too small to accommodate the guests, invited and uninvited, was supplemented by the inventive genius of Private William Chadwick, who, in the most unassuming manner, had taken control of the whole affair. He proved himself to be an invaluable aid, and his good humor gave a lightness and a zest to the occasion that would otherwise have been sadly lacking.

Under his direction the tables were arranged and the dinner set, and when the politely impatient company were summoned they found awaiting them a meal substantial enough to remind them of the old days of peace and prosperity. It was a genuine Christmas dinner. In the centre of the table there was a large bowl of egg-nog, and this was flanked and surrounded by a huge dish full of apple dumplings, a tremendous chicken pie, barbecued shote, barbecued mutton, a fat turkey, and all the various accompaniments of a country feast.

When Uncle Billy Powers had said an earnest and simple grace he gave his place at the head of the table to Colonel Watson, who had been brought in on his chair. Aunt Crissy gave Chadwick the seat of honor at the foot, and then the two old people announced that they were ready to wait on the company, with Mr. Chadwick to do the carving. If the private betrayed any embarrassment at all, he soon recovered from it.

"It ain't any use," he said, glancing down the table, "to call the roll. We're all here an' accounted for. The only man or woman that can't answer to their name is Danny Lemmons's little brown fiddle, an' I'll bet a sev'm-punce it'd skreak a little ef he tuck it out 'n the bag. But before we whirl in an' make a charge three deep, le''s begin right. This is Christmas, and that bowl yander, with the egg-nog in it, looks tired. Good as the dinner is, it's got to have a file leader. We'll start in with what looks the nighest like Christmas."

"Well," said Aunt Crissy, "I've been in sech a swivet all day I don't reelly reckon the nog is wuth your while, but you'll ha' ter take it thes like you fin' it. Hit's sweetened wi' long sweet'nin', an' it 'll ha' ter be dipped up wi' a gourd an' drunk out 'n cups."

"Lord bless you, ma'am," exclaimed Chadwick, "they won't be no questions axed ef it's got Christmas enough in it, an' I reckon it is, kaze I poured it in myself, an' I can hol' up a jug as long as the nex' man."

Though it was sweetened with syrup, the egg-nog was a success, for its strength could not be denied.

"Ef I hadn't 'a' been a prisoner of war, as you may say," remarked Chadwick, when the guests had fairly begun to discuss the dinner, "I'd 'a' got me a hunk of barbecue an' a dumplin' or two, an' a slice of that chicken pie there — I'd 'a' grabbed 'em up an' 'a' made off down the mountain. Why, I'll tell you what's the truth — I got a whiff of that barbecue by daylight, an' gentulmen, it fairly made me dribble at the mouth. Nex' to Uncle Billy there, I was the fust man at the pit."

"Yes, yes," said Uncle Billy, laughing, "that's so. An' you holp me a right smart. I'll say that."

"An' Spurlock, he got a whiff of it. Didn't you all notice, about the time he was gittin' married, how his mouth puckered up? Along towards the fust I thought he was fixin' to dip down an' give the bride a smack. But, bless you, he had barbecue on his min', an' the bride missed the buss."

"He didn't dare to buss me," exclaimed Polly, who was ministering to her grandfather. "Leastways not right out there before you all."

"Please, ma'am, don't you be skeered of Iserl," said Chadwick. "I kin take a quarter of that shote an' tole him plumb back to camp."

"Now I don't like the looks er this," exclaimed Uncle Billy Powers, who had suddenly discovered that Lovejoy, sitting by the side of Danny Lemmons, was bound so that it was impossible for him to eat in any comfort. "Come, boys, this won't do. I don't want to remember the time when any livin' human bein' sot at my table on Christmas day with his han's tied. Come, now!"

"Why, tooby shore!" exclaimed Aunt Crissy. "Turn the poor creetur loose."

"Try it!" cried Colonel Watson, in his shrill voice. "Jest try it!"

"Lord, no," said Danny Lemmons. "Look at his eyes! Look at 'em."

Lovejoy sat pale and unabashed, his eyes glittering like those of a snake. He had refused all offers of food, and seemed to be giving all his attention to Israel Spurlock.

"What does Moseley say?" asked Colonel Watson.

"Ah, he is your prisoner," said Moseley. "He never struck me as a dangerous man."

"Well," said Chadwick, "ef there's any doubt, jest take 'im out in the yard an' give 'im han'-roomance. Don't let 'im turn this table over, 'cause it 'll be a long time before some of this company 'll see the likes of it ag'in."

It was clear that Lovejoy had no friends, even among his comrades. It was clear, too, that this fact gave him no concern. He undoubtedly had more courage than his position seemed to demand. He sat glaring at Spurlock, and said never a word. Uncle Billy Powers looked at him, and gave a sigh that ended in a groan.

"Well, boys," said the old man, "this is my house, an' he's at my table. I reckon we better ontie 'im, an' let 'im git a mou'ful ter eat. 'T ain't nothin' but Christian-like."

"Don't you reckon he 'd better eat at the second table?" inquired Chadwick. This naïve suggestion provoked laughter and restored good humor, and Colonel Watson consented that Lovejoy should be released. Danny Lemmons undertook this gracious task. He had released Lovejoy's right arm, and was releasing the left, having to use his teeth on one of the knots, when the prisoner seized a fork — a large horn-handle affair, with prongs an inch and a half long — and as quick as a flash of lightning brought it down on Danny Lemmons's back. To those who happened to be looking it seemed that the fork had been plunged into the very vitals of the hunchback.

The latter went down, dragging Lovejoy after him. There was a short, sharp struggle, a heavy thump or two, and then, before the company realized what had happened, Danny Lemmons rose to his feet laughing, leaving Lovejoy lying on the floor, more securely bound than ever.

"I reckon this fork 'll have to be washed," said Danny, lifting the formidable-looking weapon from the floor.

There was more excitement after the struggle was over than there had been or could have been while it was going on. Chadwick insisted on examining Danny Lemmons's back.

"I've saw folks cut an' slashed an' stobbed before now," he explained, " an' they didn't know they was hurt tell they had done cooled off. They ain't no holes here an' they ain't no blood, but I could 'most take a right pine-blank oath that I seed 'im job that fork in your back."

"Tut, tut!" said Colonel Watson. "Do you s'pose I raised Danny Lemmons for the like of that?"

"Well," said Chadwick, resuming his seat and his dinner with unruffled nerves, temper, and appetite, "it beats the known worl'. It's the fust time I ever seed a man git down on the floor for to give the in-turn an' the under-cut, an' cut the pigeon-wing an' the double-shuffle, all before a cat could bat her eye. It looks to me that as peart a man as Lemmons there ought to be in the war."

"Ain't he in the war?" cried Colonel Watson, excitedly. "Ain't he forever and eternally in the war? Ain't he my bully bushwhacker?"

"On what side?" inquired Chadwick.

"The Union, the Union!" exclaimed the colonel, his voice rising into a scream.

"Well," said Chadwick, "ef you think you kin take the taste out'n this barbecue with talk like that, you are mighty much mistaken."

After the wedding feast was over, Danny Lemmons seized on his fiddle and made music fine enough and lively enough to set the nimble feet of the mountaineers to dancing. So that, take it all in all, the Christmas of the conscript was as jolly as he could have expected it to be.

When the festivities were concluded there was a consultation between Colonel Watson and Danny Lemmons, and then Captain Moseley and his men were told that they were free to go.

"What about Lovejoy?" asked Moseley.

"Oh, bless you! he goes over the mountain," exclaimed Danny, with a grin. "Lord, yes! Right over the mountain."

"Now, I say no," said Polly, blushing. "Turn the man loose an' let him go."

There were protests from some of the mountaineers, but Polly finally had her way. Lovejoy was unbound and permitted to go with the others, who were escorted a piece of the way down the mountain by Spurlock and some of the others. When the mountaineers started back, and before they had got out of sight, Lovejoy seized a musket from one of his men and turned and ran a little way back. What he would have done will never be known, for before he could raise his gun a streak of fire shot forth into his face, and he fell and rolled to the side of the road. An instant later Danny Lemmons leaped from the bushes, flourishing his smoking rifle.

"You see 'im now!" he cried. "You see what he was atter! He'd better have gone over the mountain. Lord, yes! Lots better."

Moseley looked at Chadwick.

"Damn him!" said the latter; "he's got what he's been a-huntin' for."

By this time the little squad of militiamen, demoralized by the incident, had fled down the mountain, and Moseley and his companion hurried after them.

ANANIAS.

I.

MIDDLE Georgia, after Sherman passed through on his famous march to the sea, was full of the direst confusion and despair, and there were many sad sights to be seen. A wide strip of country with desolate plantations, and here and there a lonely chimney standing sentinel over a pile of blackened and smouldering ruins, bore melancholy testimony to the fact that war is a very serious matter. All this is changed now, of course. The section through which the grim commander pushed his way to the sea smiles under the application of new and fresher energies. We have discovered that war, horrible as it is, sometimes drags at its bloody tumbril wheel certain fructifying and fertilizing forces. If this were not so, the contest in which the South suffered the humiliation of defeat, and more, would have been a very desperate affair indeed. The troubles of that unhappy time — its doubts, its difficulties, and its swift calamities — will never be known to posterity, for they have never been adequately described.

It was during this awful period — that is to say, in January, 1866 — that Lawyer Terrell, of Macon, made the acquaintance of his friend Ananias. In the midst of the desolation to be seen on every hand, this negro was the forlornest spectacle of all. Lawyer Terrell overtook him on the public highway between Macon and Rockville. The negro wore a ragged blue army overcoat, a pair of patched and muddy blue breeches, and had on the remmants of what was once a military cap. He was leading a lame and broken-down horse through the mud, and was making his way toward Rockville, at what appeared to be a slow and painful gait. Curiosity impelled Lawyer Terrell to draw rein as he came up with the negro.

"Howdy, boss?" said the negro, taking off his tattered cap. Responding to his salutation, the lawyer inquired his name. "I'm name' Ananias, suh," he replied.

The name seemed to fit him exactly. A meaner-looking negro Lawyer Terrell had never seen. There was not the shadow of a smile on his face, and seriousness ill became him. He had what is called a hang-dog look. A professional overseer in the old days would have regarded him as a negro to be watched, and a speculator would have put him in chains the moment he bought him. With a good deal of experience with negroes, Lawyer Terrell had never seen one whose countenance and manner were more repulsive.

"Well," said the lawyer, still keeping along with him in the muddy road, "Ananias is a good name."

"Yasser," he replied; "dat w'at mammy say. Mammy done dead now, but she say dat dey wuz two Ananiases. Dey wuz ole Ananias en young Ananias. One un um wuz de Liar, en de udder wuz de Poffit. Dat w'at mammy say. I'm name' atter de Poffit."

Lawyer Terrell laughed, and continued his cross-examination.

"Where are you going?"

"Who? Me? I'm gwine back ter Marster, suh."

"What is your master's name?"

"Cunnel Benjamime Flewellen, suh."

"Colonel Benjamin Flewellen; yes; I know the colonel well. What are you going back there for?"

"Who? Me? Dat my home, suh. I bin brung up right dar, suh — right 'longside er Marster en my young mistiss, suh."

"Miss Ellen Flewellen," said Lawyer Terrell, reflectively. At this remark the negro showed a slight interest in the conversation; but his interest did not improve his appearance.

"Yasser, dat her name, sho; but we-all call her Miss Nelly."

"A very pretty name, Ananias," remarked Lawyer Terrell.

"Lord! yasser."

The negro looked up at this, but Lawyer Terrell had his eyes fixed on the muddy road ahead of him. The lawyer was somewhat youngish himself, but his face had a hard, firm expression common to those who are in the habit of having their own way in the court-house and elsewhere.

"Where have you been, Ananias?" said the lawyer presently.

"Who? Me? I bin 'long wid Sherman army, suh."

"Then you are quite a soldier by this time."

"Lord! yasser! I bin wid um fum de time dey come in dese parts plum tell dey got ter Sander'ville. You ain't never is bin ter Sander'ville, is you, boss?"

"Not to say right in the town, Ananias, but I've been by there a great many times." Lawyer Terrell humored the conversation, as was his habit.

"Well, suh," said Ananias, "don't you never go dar; special don't you go dar wid no army, kase hit's de longes' en de nasties' road fum dar ter yer w'en you er comin' back, dat I ever is lay my two eyes on."

"Why did you come back, Ananias?"

"Who? Me? Well, suh, w'en de army come 'long by home dar, look like eve'ybody got der eye sot on me. Go whar I would, look alike all de folks wuz a-watchin' me. 'Bout time de army wuz a-pilin' in on us, Marse Wash Jones, w'ich I never is done 'im no harm dat I knows un, he went ter Marster, he did, en he 'low dat ef dey don't keep mighty close watch on Ananias dey'd all be massycreed in deir beds. I know Marse Wash tol' Marster dat, kaze Ma'y Ann, w'ich she wait on de table, she come right outer de house en tol' me so. Right den, suh, I 'gun ter feel sorter skittish. Marster had done got me ter hide all de stock out in de swamp, en I 'low ter myse'f, I did, dat I'd des go over dar en stay wid um. I ain't bin dar so mighty long, suh, w'en yer come de Yankees, en wid um wuz George, de carriage driver, de nigger w'at Marster think mo' uv dan he do all de balance er his niggers. En now, den, dar wuz George a-fetchin' de Yankees right whar he know de stock wuz hid at."

"George was a very handy negro to have around," said Lawyer Terrell.

"Yasser. Marster thunk de worl' en all er dat nigger, en dar he wuz showin' de Yankees whar de mules en hosses wuz hid at. Well, suh, soon ez he see me, George he put out, en I staid dar wid de hosses. I try ter git dem folks not ter kyar um off, I beg um en I plead wid um, but dey des laugh at me, suh. I follered 'long atter um', en dey driv dem hosses en mules right by de house. Marster wuz standin' out in de front porch, en w'en he see de Yankees got de stock, en me 'long wid um, suh, he des raise up his han's — so — en drap um down by his side, en den he tuck 'n tu'n roun' en go in de house. I run ter de do', I did, but Marster done fasten it, en den I run roun' de back way, but de back do' wuz done fassen too. I know'd dey did n't like me," Ananias went on, picking his way carefully through the mud, " en I wuz mos' out 'n my head, kaze I ain't know w'at ter do. 'Tain't wid niggers like it is wid white folks, suh. White folks know w'at ter do, kaze dey in de habits er doin' like dey wanter, but niggers, suh — niggers, dey er diffunt. Dey dunner w'at ter do."

"Well, what did you do?" asked Lawyer Terrell.

"Who? Me? Well, suh, I des crope off ter my cabin, en I draw'd up a cheer front er de fier, en stirred up de embers, en sot dar. I ain' sot dar long 'fo' Marster come ter de do'. He open it, he did, en he come in. He 'low, 'You in dar, Ananias?' I say, 'Yasser.' Den he come in. He stood dar, he did, en look at me. I ain't raise my eyes, suh; I des look in de embers. Bime-by he say, 'Ain't I allers treat you well, Ananias?' I 'low, 'Yasser.' Den he say, 'Ain't I raise you up fum a little baby, w'en you got no daddy?' I 'low, 'Yasser.' He say, 'How come you treat me dis a-way, Ananias? W'at make you show dem Yankees whar my hosses en mules is?'"

Ananias paused as he picked his way through the mud, leading his broken-down horse.

"What did you tell him?" said Lawyer Terrell, somewhat curtly.

"Well, suh, I dunner w'at de name er God come 'cross me. I wuz dat full up dat I can't talk. I tried ter tell Marster des 'zactly how it wuz, but look like I wuz all choke up. White folks kin talk right straight 'long, but niggers is diffunt. Marster stood dar, he did, en look at me right hard, en I know by de way he look dat his feelin's wuz hurted, en dis make me wuss. Eve'y time I try ter talk, suh, sumpin' ne'r kotch me in de neck, en 'fo' I kin come ter myse'f, suh, Marster wuz done gone. I got up en tried ter holler at 'im, but dat ketch wuz dar in my neck, suh, en mo' special wuz it dar, suh, w'en I see dat he wuz gwine 'long wid his head down; en dey mighty few folks, suh, dat ever is see my marster dat a-way. He kyar his head high, suh, ef I do say it myse'f."

"Why did n't you follow after him and

tell him about it?" inquired Lawyer Terrell, drawing his lap-robe closer about his knee.

"Dat des zactly w'at I oughter done, suh; but right den en dar I ain't know w'at ter do. I know'd dat nigger like me ain't got no business foolin' 'roun' much, en dat wuz all I did know. I sot down, I did, en I make up my min' dat ef Marster got de idee dat I had his stock run'd off, I better git out fum dar; en den I went ter work, suh, en I pack up w'at little duds I got, en I put out wid de army. I march wid um, suh, plum tell dey got ter Sander'ville, en dar I ax um w'at dey gwine pay me fer gwine wid um. Well, suh, you may n't b'lieve me, but dem w'ite mens dey des laugh at me. All dis time I bin runnin' over in my min' 'bout Marster en Miss Nelly, en w'en I fin' out dat dey wa'n't no pay fer niggers gwine wid de army I des up en say ter myse'f dat dat kind er business ain't gwine do fer me."

"If they had paid you anything," said Lawyer Terrell, "I suppose you would have gone on with the army?"

"Who? Me? Dat I would n't," replied Ananias, emphatically — "dat I would n't.

I 'd 'a got my money, en I 'd 'a come back home, kaze I boun' you I wa'n't a-gwine ter let Marster drap off and die widout knowin' who run'd dem stock off. No, suh. I wuz des 'bleege ter come back."

"Ananias," said Lawyer Terrell, "you are a good man."

"Thanky, suh! — thanky, marster!" exclaimed Ananias, taking off his weather-beaten cap. "You er de fus w'ite man dat ever tol' me dat sence I bin born'd inter de worl'. Thanky, suh!"

"Good-by," said Lawyer Terrell, touching his horse lightly with the whip.

"Good-by, marster!" said Ananias, with unction. "Good-by, marster! en thanky!"

Lawyer Terrell passed out of sight in the direction of Rockville. Ananias went in the same direction, but he made his way over the road with a lighter heart.

II.

It is to be presumed that Ananias's explanation was satisfactory to Colonel Benjamin Flewellen, for he settled down on his former master's place, and proceeded to make his presence felt on the farm as it never had been felt before. Himself and his army-worn horse were decided accessions, for the horse turned out to be an excellent animal. Ananias made no contract with his former master, and asked for no wages. He simply took possession of his old quarters, and began anew the life he had led in slavery times — with this difference: in the old days he had been compelled to work, but now he was working of his own free-will and to please himself. The result was that he worked much harder.

It may be said that though Colonel Benjamin Flewellen was a noted planter, he was not much of a farmer. Before and during the war he had intrusted his plantation and his planting in the care of an overseer. For three hundred dollars a year — which was not much of a sum in slavery times — he could be relieved of all the cares and anxieties incident to the management of a large plantation. His father before him had conducted the plantation by proxy, and Colonel Flewellen was not slow to avail himself of a long-established custom that had been justified by experience. Moreover, Colonel Flewellen had a taste for literature. His father had gathered together a large collection of books, and Colonel Flewellen had added to this until he was owner of one of the largest private libraries in a State where large private libraries were by no means rare. He wrote verse on occasion, and essays in defense of slavery. There are yet living men who believed that his "Reply" to Charles Sumner's attack on the South was so crushing in its argument and its invective — particularly its invective — that it would go far toward putting an end to the abolition movement. Colonel Flewellen's "Reply" filled a page of the New York "Day-Book," and there is no doubt that he made the most of the limited space placed at his disposal.

With his taste and training it is not surprising that Colonel Benjamin Flewellen should leave his plantation interests to the care of Mr. Washington Jones, his overseer, and devote himself to the liberal arts. He not only wrote and published the deservedly famous "Reply" to Charles Sumner, which was afterward reprinted in pamphlet form for the benefit of his friends and admirers, but he collected his fugitive verses in a volume, which was published by an enterprising New York firm "for the author;" and in addition to this he became the proprietor and editor of the Rockville "Vade-Mecum," a weekly paper devoted to "literature, science, politics, and the news."

When, therefore, the collapse came, the colonel found himself practically stranded. He was not only land-poor, but he had no experience in the management of his plantation. Ananias, when he returned from his jaunt with the army, was of some help, but not much. He knew how the plantation ought to be managed, but he stood in awe of the colonel, and he was somewhat backward in giving his advice. In fact, he had nothing to say unless his opinion was asked, and this was not often, for Colonel Flewellen had come to entertain the general opinion about Ananias, which was, in effect, that he was a sneaking, hypocritical rascal who was not to be depended on; a good-enough worker, to be sure, but not a negro in whom one could repose confidence.

The truth is, Ananias's appearance was against him. He was ugly and mean-looking, and he had a habit of slipping around and keeping out of the way of white people — a habit which, in that day and time, gave everybody reason enough to distrust him. As a result of this, Ananias got the credit of every mean act that could not be traced to any responsible source. If a smoke-house was broken open in the night, Ananias was the thief. The finger of suspicion was pointed at him on every possible occasion. He was thought to be the head and front of the Union League, a political organization set in motion by the shifty carpet-baggers for the purpose of consolidating the negro vote against the whites. In this way prejudice deepened against him all the while, until he finally became something of an Ishmaelite, holding no intercourse with any white people but Colonel Flewellen and Miss Nelly.

Meanwhile, as may be supposed, Colonel Flewellen was not making much of a success in managing his plantation. Beginning without money, he had as much as he could do to make "buckle and tongue meet," as the phrase goes. In fact he did not make them meet. He farmed on the old lavish plan. He borrowed money, and he bought provisions, mules, and fertilizers on credit, paying as much as two hundred per cent interest on his debts.

Strange to say, his chief creditor was Mr. Washington Jones, his former overseer. Somehow or other Mr. Jones had thrived.

He had saved money as an overseer, being a man of simple tastes and habits, and when the crash came he was comparatively a rich man. When affairs settled down somewhat, Mr. Jones blossomed out as a commission merchant, and he soon established a large and profitable business. He sold provisions and commercial fertilizers, he bought cotton, and he was not above any transaction, however small, that promised to bring him a dime where he had invested a thrip. He was a very thrifty man indeed. In addition to his other business he shaved notes and bought mortgages, and in this way the fact came to be recognized, as early as 1868, that he was what is known as "a leading citizen." He did not hesitate to grind a man when he had him in his clutches, and on this account he made enemies; but as his worldly possessions grew and assumed tangible proportions, it is not to be denied that he had more friends than enemies.

For a while Mr. Washington Jones's most prominent patron was Colonel Benjamin Flewellen. The colonel, it should be said, was not only a patron of Jones, but he patronized him. He made his purchases, chiefly on credit, in a lordly, superior way, as became a gentleman whose hireling Jones had been. When the colonel had money he was glad to pay cash for his supplies, but it happened somehow that he rarely had money. Jones, it must be confessed, was very accommodating. He was anxious to sell to the colonel on the easiest terms, so far as payment was concerned, and he often, in a sly way, flattered the colonel into making larger bills than he otherwise would have made.

There could be but one result, and though that result was inevitable, everybody about Rockville seemed to be surprised. The colonel had disposed of his newspaper long before, and one day there appeared, in the columns which he had once edited with such care, a legal notice to the effect that he had applied to the ordinary of the county, in proper form, to set aside a homestead and personalty. This meant that the colonel, with his old-fashioned ways and methods, had succumbed to the inevitable. He had a house and lot in town, and this was set apart as his homestead by the judge of ordinary. Mr. Washington Jones, you may be sure, lost no time in foreclosing his mortgages, and the fact soon came to be known that he was now the proprietor of the Flewellen place.

Just at this point the colonel first began to face the real problems of life, and he found them to be very knotty ones. He must live — but how? He knew no law, and was acquainted with no business. He was a gentleman and a scholar; but these accomplishments would not serve him; indeed, they stood in his way. He had been brought up to no business, and it was a little late in life — the colonel was fifty or more — to begin to learn. He might have entered upon a political career, and this would have been greatly to his taste, but all the local offices were filled by competent men, and just at that time a Southerner to the manner born had little chance to gain admission to Congress. The Republican "reconstructionists," headed by Thaddeus Stevens, barred the way. The outlook was gloomy indeed.

Nelly Flewellen, who had grown to be a beautiful woman, and who was as accomplished as she was beautiful, gave music lessons; but in Rockville at that time there was not much to be made by teaching music. It is due to the colonel to say that he was bitterly opposed to this project, and he was glad when his daughter gave it up in despair. Then she took in sewing surreptitiously, and did other things that a girl of tact and common sense would be likely to do when put to the test.

The colonel and his daughter managed to get along somehow, but it was a miserable existence compared to their former estate of luxury. Just how they managed, only one person in the wide world knew, and that person was Ananias. Everybody around Rockville said it was very queer how the colonel, with no money and little credit, could afford to keep a servant, and a man-servant at that. But there was nothing queer about it. Ananias received no wages of any sort; he asked for none; he expected none. A child of misfortune himself, he was glad to share the misfortunes of his former master. He washed, he ironed, he cooked, he milked, and he did more. He found time to do little odd jobs around town, and with the money thus earned he was able to supply things that would otherwise have been missing from Colonel Flewellen's table. He was as ugly and as mean-looking as ever, and as unpopular. Even the colonel distrusted him, but he managed to tolerate him. The daughter often had words of praise for the shabby and forlorn-looking negro, and these, if anything, served to lighten his tasks.

But in spite of everything that his daughter or Ananias could do, the colonel continued to grow poorer. To all appearances — and he managed to keep up appearances to the last — he was richer than many of his neighbors, for he had a comfortable house, and he still had credit in the town. Among the shopkeepers there were few that did not respect and admire the colonel for what he had been. But the colonel, since his experience with Mr. Washington Jones, looked with suspicion on the credit business. The result was that he and his daughter and Ananias lived in the midst of the ghastliest poverty.

As for Ananias, he could stand it well enough; so, perhaps, could the colonel, he being a man, and a pretty stout one; but how about the young lady? This was the question that Ananias was continually asking himself, and circumstances finally drove him to answering it in his own way. There was this much to be said about Ananias;

when he made up his mind, nothing could turn him, humble as he was; and then came a period in the career of the family to which he had attached himself when he was compelled to make up his mind or see them starve.

III.

At this late day there is no particular reason for concealing the facts. Ananias took the responsibility on his shoulders, and thereafter the colonel's larder was always comparatively full. At night Ananias would sit and nod before a fire in the kitchen, and after everybody else had gone to bed he would sneak out into the darkness, and be gone for many hours; but whether the hours of his absence were many or few, he never returned empty-handed. Sometimes he would bring a "turn" of wood, sometimes a bag of meal or potatoes, sometimes a side of meat or a ham, and sometimes he would be compelled to stop, while yet some distance from the house, to choke a chicken that betrayed a tendency to squall in the small still hours between midnight and morning. The colonel and his daughter never knew whence their supplies came. They only knew that Ananias suddenly developed into a wonderfully good cook, for it is a very good cook indeed that can go on month after month providing excellent meals without calling for new supplies.

But Ananias had always been peculiar, and if he grew a trifle more uncommunicative than usual, neither the colonel nor the colonel's daughter was expected to take notice of the fact. Ananias was a sullen negro at best, but his sullenness was not at all important, and nobody cared whether his demeanor was grave or gay, lively or severe. Indeed, except that he was an object of distrust and suspicion, nobody cared anything at all about Ananias. For his part, Ananias seemed to care nothing for people's opinions, good, bad, or indifferent. If the citizens of Rockville thought ill of him, that was their affair altogether. Ananias went sneaking around, attending to what he conceived to be his own business, and there is no doubt that, in some way, he managed to keep Colonel Flewellen's larder well supplied with provisions.

About this time Mr. Washington Jones, who had hired a clerk for his store, and who was mainly devoting his time to managing, as proprietor, the Flewellen place, which he had formerly managed as overseer, began to discover that he was the victim of a series of mysterious robberies and burglaries. Nobody suffered but Mr. Jones, and everybody said that it was not only very unjust, but very provoking also, that this enterprising citizen should be systematically robbed, while all his neighbors should escape. These mysterious robberies soon became the talk of the whole county. Some people sympathized with Jones, while others laughed at him. Certainly the mystery was a very funny mystery, for when Jones watched his potato hill, his smoke-house was sure to be entered. If he watched his smoke-house, his potato hill would suffer. If he divided his time watching both of these, his store-house would be robbed. There was no regularity about this; but it was generally conceded that the more Jones watched, the more he was robbed, and it finally came to be believed in the county that Jones, to express it in the vernacular, "hollered too loud to be hurt much."

At last one day it was announced that Jones had discovered the thief who had been robbing him. He had not caught him, but he had seen him plainly enough to identify him. The next thing that Rockville knew, a warrant had been issued for Ananias, and he was arrested. He had no commitment trial. He was lodged in the jail to await trial in the Superior Court. Colonel Flewellen was sorry for the negro, as well he might be, but he was afraid to go on his bond. Faithful as Ananias had been, he was a negro, after all, the colonel argued, and if he was released on bond he would not hesitate to run away, if such an idea should occur to him.

Fortunately for Ananias, he was not permitted to languish in jail. The Superior Court met the week after he was arrested, and his case was among the first called. It seemed to be a case, indeed, that needed very little trying. But a very curious incident happened in the court-room.

Among the lawyers present was Mr. Terrell, of Macon. Mr. Terrell was by all odds the greatest lawyer practising in that circuit. He was so great, indeed, that he was not called "major," or "colonel," or "judge." He ranked with Stephens and Hill, and like these distinguished men his title was plain "Mr." Mr. Terrell practised in all the judicial circuits of the State, and had important cases in all of them. He was in Rockville for the purpose of arguing a case to be tried at term, and which he knew would be carried to the Supreme Court of the State, no matter what the verdict of the lower court might be. He was arranging and verifying his authorities anew, and he was very busy when the sheriff came into the court-house bringing Ananias. The judge on the bench thought he had never seen a more rascally-looking prisoner; but even rascally-looking prisoners have their rights, and so, when Ananias's case was called, the judge asked him in a friendly way if he had counsel — if he had engaged a lawyer to defend him.

Ananias did not understand at first, but when the matter was made plain to him he said he could get a lawyer. Whereupon he walked over to where Mr. Terrell sat immersed in his big books, and touched him on the shoulder. The lawyer looked up.

"I'm name' Ananias, suh," said the negro.

"I remember you," said Mr. Terrell. "What are you doing here?"

"Dey got me up fer my trial, suh, en I

'ain't got nobody fer ter speak de word fer me, suh, en I 'low'd maybe — "

Ananias paused. He knew not what else to say. He had no sort of claim on this man. He saw everybody around him laughing. The great lawyer himself smiled as he twirled his eye-glasses on his fingers. Ananias was embarrassed.

"You want me to speak the word?" said Mr. Terrell.

"Yes, suh, if you please, suh."

"You need not trouble yourself, Mr. Terrell," said the judge, affably. "I was about to appoint counsel."

"May it please your honor," said Mr. Terrell, rising. "I will defend this boy. I know nothing whatever of the case, but I happen to know something of the negro."

There was quite a little stir in the court-room at this announcement. The loafers outside the railings of the bar, who had seen Ananias every day for a good many years, leaned forward to take another look at him. The lawyers inside the bar also seemed to be interested in the matter. Some thought that the great lawyer had taken the negro's case by way of a joke, and they promised themselves a good deal of enjoyment, for it is not every day that a prominent man is seen at play. Others knew not what to think; so that between those who regarded it as a practical joke and those who thought that Mr. Terrell might be in a serious mood, the affair caused quite a sensation.

"May it please the court," said Mr. Terrell, his firm voice penetrating to every part of the large room, "I know nothing of this case; therefore I will ask half an hour's delay to look over the papers and to consult with my client."

"Certainly," said the judge, pleasantly. "Mr. Sheriff, take the prisoner to the Grand Jury room, so that he may consult with his counsel."

The sheriff locked the prisoner and the lawyer in the Grand Jury room, and left his deputy there to open the door when Mr. Terrell announced that the conference was over. In the mean time the court proceeded with other business. Cases were settled, dismissed, or postponed. A couple of young lawyers fell into a tumultuous wrangle over an immaterial point, which the judge disposed of with a wave of his hand.

In the Grand Jury room Ananias was telling his volunteer counsel a strange tale.

IV.

"And do you mean to tell me that you really stole these things from Jones?" said Mr. Terrell, after he had talked a little with his client.

"Well, suh," replied Ananias, unabashed, "I did n't zackly steal um, suh, but I tuck um; I des tuck um, suh."

"What call had you to steal from Jones? Were n't you working for Colonel Flewellen? Did n't he feed you?" inquired the lawyer. Ananias shifted about from one foot to the other, and whipped his legs with his shabby hat, which he held in his hand. Lawyer Terrell, seated in a comfortable chair, and thoroughly at his ease, regarded the negro curiously. There appeared to be a pathetic element even in Ananias's manner.

"Well, suh," he said, after a while, seeing that he could not escape from the confession, "ef I had n't a-tuck dem things fum Marse Wash Jones, my Marster en my young mistiss would 'a sot dar en bodaciously starve deyse'f ter deff. I done seed dat, suh. Dey wuz too proud ter tell folks dey wuz dat bad off, suh, en dey 'd 'a sot dar, en des bodaciously starve deyse'f ter deff, suh. All dey lifetime, suh, dey bin use ter havin' deir vittles put right on de table whar dey kin git it, en w'en de farmin' days done gone, suh, dey wa'n't nobody but Ananias fer put de vittles dar; en I des hatter scuffle 'roun' en git it de bes' way I kin. I 'spec', suh," Ananias went on, his countenance brightening up a little, "dat ef de wuss had a-come ter de wuss, I 'd 'a' stole de vittles; but I 'ain't had ter steal it, suh; I des went en tuck it fum Marse Wash Jones, kaze it come off'n Marster's lan', suh."

"Why, the land belongs to Jones," said Lawyer Terrell.

"Dat w'at dey say, suh; but eve'y foot er dat lan' b'longded ter de Flewellen fambly long 'fo' Marse Wash Jones' daddy sot up a hat-shop in de neighborhoods. I dunner how Marse Wash git dat lan', suh; I know it b'longded in de Flewellen fambly sence 'way back, en dey got deir graveyard dar yit."

Lawyer Terrell's unusually stern face softened a little. He saw that Ananias was in earnest, and his sympathies were aroused. He had some further conversation with the negro, questioning him in regard to a great many things that assumed importance in the trial.

When Lawyer Terrell and his client returned to the court-room they found it filled with spectators. Somehow, it became generally known that the great advocate was to defend Ananias, and a large crowd of people had assembled to watch developments. In some way the progress of Ananias and the deputy-sheriff through the crowd that filled all the aisles and doorways had been delayed; but when the negro, forlorn and wretched-looking, made his appearance in the bar for the purpose of taking a seat by his counsel, there was a general laugh. Instantly Lawyer Terrell was upon his feet.

"May it please your honor, what *is* the duty of the sheriff of this county, if it is not to keep order in this court-room?"

The ponderous staff of the sheriff came down on the floor with a thump; but it was unnecessary. Silence had fallen on the spectators with the first words of the lawyer. The crowd knew that he was a game man, and they admired him for it. His whole attitude, as he gazed at the people around him, showed that he was full of fight. His heavy blond hair, swept back from his high forehead, looked like the mane of a lion, and his steel-gray eyes glittered under his shaggy and frowning brows.

The case of the State *versus* Ananias Flewellen, *alias* Ananias Harper — a name he had taken since freedom — was called in due form. It was observed that Lawyer Terrell was very particular to strike certain names from the jury list, but this gave no cue to the line of his defense. The first witness was Mr. Washington Jones, who detailed, as well as he knew how, the circumstances of the various robberies of which he had been the victim. He had suspected Ananias, but had not made his suspicions known until he was sure, — until he had caught him stealing sweet-potatoes.

The cross-examination of the witness by Ananias's counsel was severe. The fact was gradually developed that Mr. Jones caught the negro stealing potatoes at night; that the night was dark and cloudy; that he did not actually catch the negro, but saw him; that he did not really see the negro clearly, but knew "in reason" that it must be Ananias.

The fact was also developed that Mr.

Jones was not alone when he saw Ananias, but was accompanied by Mr. Miles Cottingham, a small farmer in the neighborhood, who was well known all over the county as a man of undoubted veracity and of the strictest integrity.

At this point Lawyer Terrell, who had been facing Mr. Jones with severity painted on his countenance, seemed suddenly to recover his temper. He turned to the listening crowd, and said, in his blandest tones, "Is Mr. Miles Cottingham in the room?"

There was a pause, and then a small boy perched in one of the windows, through which the sun was streaming, cried out, "He's a-standin' out yander by the horse-rack."

Whereupon a subpœna was promptly made out by the clerk of the court, and the deputy sheriff, putting his head out of a window, cried:

"Miles G. Cottingham! Miles G. Cottingham! Miles G. Cottingham! Come into court."

Mr. Cottingham was fat, rosy, and cheerful. He came into court with such a dubious smile on his face that his friends in the room were disposed to laugh, but they remembered that Lawyer Terrell was somewhat intolerant of these manifestations of good-humor. As for Mr. Cottingham himself, he was greatly puzzled. When the voice of the court crier reached his ears he was in the act of taking a dram, and, as he said afterward, he "come mighty nigh drappin' the tumbeler." But he was not subjected to any such mortification. He tossed off his dram in fine style, and went to the court-house, where, as soon as he had pushed his way to the front, he was met by Lawyer Terrell, who shook him heartily by the hand, and told him his testimony was needed in order that justice might be done.

Then Mr. Cottingham was put on the stand as a witness for the defense.

"How old are you, Mr. Cottingham?" said Lawyer Terrell.

"Ef I make no mistakes, I'm a-gwine on sixty-nine," replied the witness.

"Are your eyes good?"

"Well, sir, they er about ez good ez the common run; not so good ez they mought be, en yit good enough fer me."

"Did you ever see that negro before?" The lawyer pointed to Ananias.

"Which nigger? That un over there?

Why, that's thish yer God-forsakin' Ananias. Ef it had a-bin any yuther nigger but Ananias I would n't 'a' bin so certain and shore; bekaze sence the war they er all so mighty nigh alike I can't tell one from t'other sca'cely. All eckceppin' of Ananias; I'd know Ananias ef I met 'im in kingdom come wi' his hair all swinjed off."

The jury betrayed symptoms of enjoying this testimony; seeing which, the State's attorney rose to his feet to protest.

"May it please the court" —

"One moment, your honor!" exclaimed Lawyer Terrell. Then, turning to the witness: "Mr. Cottingham, were you with Mr. Jones when he was watching to catch a thief who had been stealing from him?"

"Well, sir," replied Mr. Cottingham, "I sot up wi' him one night, but I disremember in pertickler what night it wuz."

"Did you see the thief?"

"Well, sir," said Mr. Cottingham, in his deliberate way, looking around over the court-room with a more judicial air than the judge on the bench, "ef you push me close I'll tell you. Ther wuz a consid'able flutterment in the neighborhoods er whar we sot, an' me an' Wash done some mighty sly slippin' up en surrounderin'; but ez ter seein' anybody, we did n't see 'im. We heerd 'm a-scufflin' an' a-runnin', but we did n't ketch a glimpse un 'im, nuther har ner hide."

"Did Mr. Jones see him?"

"No more 'n I did. I wuz right at Wash's elbow. We heerd the villyun a-runnin', but we never seed 'im. Atterwards, when we got back ter the house, Wash he 'lowed it must 'a bin that nigger Ananias thar, an' I 'lowed it jess mought ez well be Ananias ez any yuther nigger, bekaze you know yourself — "

"That will do, Mr. Cottingham," said Mr. Lawyer Terrell, blandly. The State's attorney undertook to cross-examine Mr. Cottingham; but he was a blundering man, and the result of his cross-examination was simply a stronger and more impressive repetition of Mr. Cottingham's testimony.

After this, the solicitor was willing to submit the case to the jury without argument, but Mr. Terrell said that if it pleased the court he had a few words to say to the jury in behalf of his client. The speech made by the State's attorney was flat and stale, for he was not interested in the case; but Lawyer Terrell's appeal to the jury is still remembered in Rockville. It was not only powerful, but inimitable; it was humorous, pathetic, and eloquent. When he concluded, the jury, which was composed mostly of middle-aged men, was in tears. The feelings of the spectators were also wrought up to a very high pitch, and when the jury found a verdict of "not guilty," without retiring, the people in the court-room made the old house ring again with applause.

And then something else occurred. Pressing forward through the crowd came Colonel Benjamin Flewellen. His clothes were a trifle shabby, but he had the air of a prince of the blood. His long white hair fell on his shoulders, and his movements were as precise as those of a grenadier. The spectators made way for him. Those nearest noticed that his eyes were moist, and that his nether lip was a-tremble, but no one made any remark. Colonel Flewellen pressed forward until he reached Ananias, who, scarcely comprehending the situation, was sitting with his hands folded and his head bent down. The colonel placed his hand on the negro's shoulder.

"Come, boy," he said, "let 's go home."

"Me, Marster?" said the negro, looking

up with a dazed expression. It was the tone, and not the words, that Ananias heard.

"Yes, old fellow, your Miss Nelly will be waiting for us."

"Name er God!" exclaimed Ananias, and then he arose and followed his old master out of the court-room. Those who watched him as he went saw that the tears were streaming down his face, but there was no rude laughter when he made a futile attempt to wipe them off with his coat-tail. This display of feeling on the part of the negro was somewhat surprising to those who witnessed it, but nobody was surprised when Ananias appeared on the streets a few days after with head erect and happiness in his face.

WHERE'S DUNCAN?

Now, do you know you young people are mighty queer? Somebody has told you that he heard old man Isaiah Winchell a-gabbling about old times, and here you come fishing for what you call a story. Why, bless your soul, man, it is no story at all, just a happening, as my wife used to say. If you want me to tell what there is of it, there must be some understanding about it. You know what ought to be put in print and what ought to be left out. I would know myself, I reckon, if I stopped to think it all over; but there's the trouble. When I get started, I just rattle along like a runaway horse. I'm all motion and no sense, and there's no stopping me until I run over a stump or up against a fence. And if I tried to write it out, it would be pretty much the same. When I take a pen in my hand my mind takes all sorts of uncertain flights, like a pigeon with a hawk after it.

As to the affair you were speaking of, there's not much to tell, but it has pestered me at times when I ought to have been in my bed and sound asleep. I have told it a thousand times, and the rest of the Winchells have told it, thinking it was a very good thing to have in the family. It has been exaggerated, too; but if I can carry the facts to your ear just as they are in my mind, I shall be glad, for I want to get everything straight from the beginning.

Well, it was in 1826. That seems a long time ago to you, but it is no longer than yesterday to me. I was eighteen years old, and a right smart chunk of a boy for my age. While we were ginning and packing cotton our overseer left us, and my father turned the whole business over to me. Now, you may think that was a small thing, because this railroad business has turned your head, but, as a matter of fact, it was a very big thing. It fell to me to superintend the ginning and the packing of the cotton, and then I was to go to Augusta in charge of two wagons. I never worked harder before nor since. You see we had no packing-screws nor cotton-presses in those days. The planter that was able to afford it had his gin, and the cotton was packed in round bales by a nigger who used something like a crowbar to do the packing. He trampled the lint cotton with his feet, and beat it down with his iron bar until the bagging was full, and then the bale weighed about three hundred pounds. Naturally you laugh at this sort of thing, but it was no laughing matter; it was hard work.

Well, when we got the cotton all prepared, we loaded the wagons and started for Augusta. We had n't got more than two miles from home, before I found that Crooked-leg Jake, my best driver, was drunk. He was beastly drunk. Where he got his dram, I could n't tell you to save my life, for it was against the law in those days to sell whiskey to a nigger. But Crooked-leg Jake had it and he was full of it, and he had to be pulled off of the mule and sent to roost on top of the cotton-bags. It was not a very warm roost either, but it was warm enough for a nigger full of whiskey.

This was not a good thing for me at all, but I had to make the best of it. Moreover, I had to do what I had never done before — I had to drive six mules, and there was only one rein to drive them with. This was the fashion, but it was a very difficult matter for a youngster to get the hang of it. You jerk, jerk, jerked, if you wanted the lead mule to turn to the right, and you pull, pull, pulled if you wanted her to go the left. While we were going on in this way, with a stubborn mule at the wheel and a drunken nigger on the wagon, suddenly there came out of the woods a thick-set, dark-featured, black-bearded man with a bag slung across his shoulder.

"Hello!" says he; "you must be a new hand."

"It would take a very old hand," said I, "to train a team of mules to meet you in the road."

"Now, there you have me," said he; and he laughed as if he were enjoying a very good joke.

"Who hitched up your team?" he asked.

"That drunken nigger," said I.

"To be sure," said he; "I might have known it. The lead-mule is on the off side."

"Why, how do you know that?" I asked.

"My two eyes tell me," he replied; "they are pulling crossways." And with that, without asking anybody's permission,

he unhitched the traces, unbuckled the reins
and changed the places of the two front
mules. It was all done in a jiffy, and in
such a light-hearted manner that no protest
could be made; and, indeed, no protest was
necessary, for the moment the team started
I could see that the stranger was right.
There was no more jerking and whipping to
be done. We went on in this way for a
mile or more, when suddenly I thought to
ask the stranger, who was trudging along
good-humoredly by the side of the wagon, if
he would like to ride. He laughed and said
he would n't mind it if I would let him
straddle the saddle-mule; and for my part I
had no objections.

So I crawled up on the cotton and lay
there with Crooked-leg Jake. I had been
there only a short time when the nigger
awoke and saw me. He looked scared.

"Who dat drivin' dem mules, Marse
Isaiah?" he asked.

"I could n't tell you even if you were
sober," said I. "The lead-mule was hitched
on the off-side, and the man that is driving
rushed out of the woods, fixed her right, and
since then we have been making good time."

"Is he a sho' 'nuff w'ite man, Marse
Isaiah?" asked Jake.

"Well, he looks like he is," said I; "but I'm not certain about that."

With that Jake crawled to the front of the wagon, and looked over at the driver. After a while he came crawling back.

"Tell me what you saw," said I.

"Well, sir," said he, "I dunner whe'er dat man's a w'ite man or not, but he's a-settin' sideways on dat saddle-mule, en every time he chirps, dat lead-mule know what he talkin' about. Yasser. She do dat. Did you say he come outen de woods?"

"I don't know where he came from," said I. "He's there, and he's driving the mules."

"Yasser. Dat's so. He's dar sho', kaze I seed 'im wid my own eyes. He look like he made outen flesh en blood, en yit he mought be a ha'nt; dey ain't no tellin'. Dem dar mules is gwine on mos' too slick fer ter suit me."

Well, the upshot of it was that the stranger continued to drive. He made himself useful during the day, and when night came, he made himself musical; for in the pack slung across his back was a fiddle, and in the manipulation of this instrument he showed a power and a mastery which are given to few men to possess. I doubt whether he would have made much of a show on the stage, but I have heard some of your modern players, and none of them could approach him, according to my taste. I'll tell you why. They all seem to play the music for the music itself, but this man played it for the sake of what it reminded him of. I remember that when he took out his fiddle at night, as he invariably did if nobody asked him to, I used to shut my eyes and dream dreams that I have never dreamed since, and see visions that are given to few men to see. If I were younger I could describe it to you, but an old man like me is not apt at such descriptions.

We journeyed on, and, as we journeyed, we were joined by other wagons hauling cotton, until, at last, there was quite a caravan of them — twenty, at least, and possibly more. This made matters very lively, as you may suppose, especially at night, when we went into camp. Then there were scenes such as have never been described in any of the books that profess to tell about life in the South before the war. After the teams had been fed and supper cooked, the niggers would sing, dance and wrestle, and the white men would gather to egg them on, or sit by their fires and tell stories or play cards. Sometimes there would be a fight, and that was exciting; for in those days, the shotgun was mighty handy and the dirk was usually within reach. In fact, there was every amusement that such a crowd of people could manage to squeeze out of such an occasion. In our caravan there were more than a dozen fiddlers, white and black, but not one of them that attracted as much attention as the stranger who drove my team. When he was in the humor he could entrance the whole camp; but it was not often that he would play, and it frequently happened that he and I would go to bed under our wagon while the rest of the teamsters were frolicking. I had discovered that he was a good man to have along. He knew just how to handle the mules, he knew all the roads, he knew just where to camp, and he knew how to keep Crooked-leg Jake sober. One night after we had gone to bed he raised himself on his elbow and said:

"To-morrow night, if I make no mistake, we will camp within a few miles of the Sandhills. There my journey ends, and yet you have never asked me my name."

"Well," said I, "you are a much older man than I am, and I had a notion that if you wanted me to know your name you would tell me. I had no more reason for asking it than you have for hiding it."

He lay over on his back and laughed.

"You'll find out better than that when you are older," he said, and then he continued laughing — though whether it was what I said or his own thoughts that tickled him, I had no means of knowing.

"Well," he went on, after a while, "you are as clever a youngster as ever I met, and I've nothing to hide from you. My name is Willis Featherstone, and I am simply a vagabond, else you would never have seen me trudging along the public road with only a fiddle at my back; but I have a rich daddy hereabouts, and I'm on my way to see how he is getting along. Now," he continued, "I'll give you a riddle. If you can't unriddle it, it will unriddle itself. A father had a son. He sent him to school in Augusta, until he was fifteen. By that time, the father grew to hate the son, and one day, in a fit of anger, sold him to a nigger speculator."

"How could that be?" I asked.

"That is a part of the riddle," said he.

"Are you the son?"

"That is another part of the same riddle."

"Where was the son's mother?" I asked.

"In the riddle — in the riddle," replied.

I could not unriddle the riddle, but it seemed to hint at some such villainy as I had read about in the books in my father's library. Here was a man who had sold his son; that was enough for me. It gave me matter to dream on, and as I was a pretty heavy feeder in those days, my dreams followed hard on each other. But it isn't worth while to relate them here, for the things that actually happened were infinitely worse than any dream could be.

As Featherstone had foretold, we camped the next night not far from the Sandhills, where the rich people of Augusta went every summer to escape the heat and malaria of the city. We might have gone on and reached Augusta during the night, but both men and mules were tired, and of the entire caravan only one wagon went forward. I shall remember the place as long as I live. In a little hollow, surrounded by live-oaks —

we call them water-oaks up here — was a
very bold spring, and around and about was
plenty of grass for the mules. It was somewhat dry, the time being November, but it
made excellent forage. On a little hill beyond the spring was a dwelling-house. I
came to have a pretty good view of it afterward, but in the twilight it seemed to be a
very substantial building. It was painted
white and had green blinds, and it sat in
the midst of a beautiful grove of magnolias
and cedars. I remember, too, — it is all
impressed on my mind so vividly — that the
avenue leading to the house was lined on
each side with Lombardy poplars, and their
spindling trunks stood clearly out against
the sky.

While I was helping Featherstone un-
hitch and unharness the mules, he suddenly
remarked: —

"That's the place."

"What place?" I asked.

"The place the riddle tells about —
where the son was sold by his father."

"Well," said I, by way of saying something, "what can't be cured must be endured."

"You are a very clever chap," he said,

after a while. "In fact you are the best chap I have seen for many a long day, and I like you. I've watched you like a hawk, and I know you have a mother at home."

"Yes," said I, "and she's the dearest old mother you ever saw. I wish you knew her."

He came up to me, laid his hand on my shoulder, and looked into my face with an air I can never forget.

"That is the trouble," said he; "I don't know her. If I did I would be a better man. I never had much of a mother."

With that he turned away, and soon I heard him singing softly to himself as he mended a piece of the harness. All this time Crooked-leg Jake was cooking our supper beneath the live-oak trees. Other teamsters were doing the same, so that there were two dozen camp-fires burning brightly within an area of not more than a quarter of a mile. The weather was pleasant, too, and the whole scene struck me as particularly lively.

Crooked-leg Jake was always free-handed with his cooking. He went at it with a zest born of his own insatiate appetite, and it was not long before we were through with it; and while the other campers were fuming and stewing over their cooking, Jake was sitting by the fire nodding, and Featherstone was playing his fiddle. He never played it better than he did that night, and he played it a long time, while I sat listening. Meanwhile quite a number of the teamsters gathered around, some reclining in the leaves smoking their pipes, and others standing around in various positions. Suddenly I discovered that Featherstone had a new and an unexpected auditor. Just how I discovered this I do not know; it must have been proned in upon me, as the niggers say. I observed that he gripped the neck of his fiddle a little tighter, and suddenly he swung off from "Money-musk" into one of those queer serenades which you have heard now and again on the plantation. Where the niggers ever picked up such tunes the Lord only knows, but they are heart-breaking ones.

Following the glance of Featherstone's eyes, I looked around, and I saw, standing within the circle of teamsters, a tall mulatto woman. She was a striking figure as she stood there gazing with all her eyes, and listening with all her ears. Her hair was black and straight as that of an Indian, her cheeks were sunken, and there was that in her countenance that gave her a wolfish aspect. As she stood there rubbing her skinny hands together and moistening her thin lips with her tongue, she looked like one distraught. When Featherstone stopped playing, pretending to be tuning his fiddle, the mulatto woman drew a long breath, and made an effort to smile. Her thin lips fell apart and her white teeth gleamed in the firelight like so many fangs. Finally she spoke, and it was an ungracious speech: —

"Ole Giles Featherstone, up yonder — he's my marster — he sont me down here an' tole me to tell you-all dat, bein 's he got some vittles lef' over fum dinner, he'll be glad ef some un you would come take supper 'long wid 'im. But, gentermens" — here she lowered her voice, giving it a most tragic tone — "you better not go, kaze he ain't got nothin' up dar dat's fittin' ter eat — some cole scraps an' de frame uv a turkey. He scrimps hisse'f, an' he scrimps me, an' he scrimps eve'ybody on de place, an' he'll scrimp you-all ef you go dar. No, gentermens, ef you des got corn-bread an' bacon you better stay 'way."

Whatever response the teamsters might have made was drowned by Featherstone's fiddle, which plunged suddenly into the wild and plaintive strains of a plantation melody. The mulatto woman stood like one entranced; she caught her breath, drew back a few steps, stretched forth her ebony arms, and cried out: —

"Who de name er God is dat man?"

With that Featherstone stopped his playing, fixed his eyes on the woman, and exclaimed: —

"*Where's Duncan?*"

For a moment the woman stood like one paralyzed. She gasped for breath, her arms jerked convulsively, and there was a twitching of the muscles of her face pitiful to behold; then she rushed forward and fell on her knees at the fiddler's feet, hugging his legs with her arms.

"Honey, who is you?" she cried in a loud voice. "In de name er de Lord, who is you! Does you know me? Say, honey, does you?"

Featherstone looked at the writhing woman serenely.

"Come, now," he said, "I ask you once more, *Where's Duncan?*"

His tone was most peculiar: it was thrilling, indeed, and it had a tremendous effect on the woman. She rose to her feet, flung her bony arms above her head, and ran off into the darkness, screaming: —

"He sold 'im! — he sold Duncan! He sold my onliest boy!"

This she kept on repeating as she ran, and her voice died away like an echo in the direction of the house on the hill. There was not much joking among the teamsters over this episode, and somehow there was very little talk of any kind. None of us accepted the invitation. Featherstone put his fiddle in his bag, and walked off toward the wagons, and it was not long before everybody had turned in for the night.

I suppose I had been asleep an hour when I felt some one shaking me by the shoulder. It was Crooked-leg Jake.

"Marse Isaiah," said he, "dey er cuttin' up a mighty rippit up dar at dat house on de hill. I 'spec' somebody better go up dar."

"What are they doing?" I asked him drowsily.

"Dey er cussin' an' gwine on scan'lous. Dat ar nigger 'oman, she's a-cussin' out de white man, an' de white man, he's a-cussin' back at her."

"Where's Featherstone?" I inquired, still not more than half awake.

"Dat what make me come atter you, suh. Dat white man what bin 'long wid us, he's up dar, an' it look like ter me dat he's a-aggin' de fuss on. Dey gwine ter be trouble up dar, sho ez you er born."

"Bosh!" said I, "the woman's master will call her up, give her a strapping, and that will be the end of it."

"No, suh! no, suh!" exclaimed Jake; "dat ar nigger 'oman done got dat white man hacked. Hit's des like I tell you, mon!"

I drove Jake off to bed, turned over on my pallet, and was about to go to sleep again, when I heard quite a stir in the camp. The mules and horses were snorting and tugging at their halters, the chickens on the hill were cackling, and somewhere near, a flock of geese was screaming. Just then Crooked-leg Jake came and shook me by the shoulder again. I spoke to him somewhat sharply, but he didn't seem to mind it.

"What I tell you, Marse Isaiah?" he cried. "Look up yonder! Ef dat house ain't afire on top, den Jake's a liar!"

I turned on my elbow, and, sure enough, the house on the hill was outlined in flame. The hungry, yellow tongues of fire reached up the corners and ran along the roof, lapping the shingles, here and there, as if blindly searching for food. They found it, too, for by the time I reached the spot, and you may be sure I was not long getting there, the whole roof was in a blaze. I had never seen a house on fire before, and the sight of it made me quake; but in a moment I had forgotten all about the fire, for there, right before my eyes, was a spectacle that will haunt me to my dying day. In the dining-room — I suppose it must have been the dining-room, for there was a sideboard with a row of candles on it — I saw the mulatto woman (the same that had acted so queerly when Featherstone had asked her about Duncan) engaged in an encounter with a gray-haired white man. The candles on the sideboard and the flaring flames without lit up the affair until it looked like some of the spectacles I have since seen in theatres, only it was more terrible.

It was plain that the old man was no match for the woman, but he fought manfully for his life. Whatever noise they made must have been drowned by the crackling and roaring of the flames outside; but they seemed to be making none except a snarling sound when they caught their breath, like two bull-dogs fighting. The woman had a carving-knife in her right hand, and she was endeavoring to push the white man against the wall. He, on his side, was trying to catch and hold the hand in which the woman held the knife, and was also making a frantic effort to keep away from the wall. But the woman had the advantage; she was younger and stronger, and desperate as he was, she was more desperate still.

Of course, it is a very easy matter to ask why some of my companions or myself did n't rush to the rescue. I think such an attempt was made; but the roof of the house was ablaze and crackling from one end to the other, and the heat and smoke were stifling. The smoke and flames, instead of springing upward, ranged downward, so that before anything could be done, the building appeared to be a solid sheet of fire; but through it all could be seen the writhing and wrestling of the nigger woman and the white man. Once, and only once, did I catch the sound of a voice; it was the voice of the nigger woman; she had her carving-knife raised in the air in one hand, and with the other she had the white man by the throat.

"*Where's Duncan?*" she shrieked.

If the man had been disposed to reply, he had no opportunity, for the woman had no sooner asked the question than she plunged the carving-knife into his body, not only once, but twice. It was a sickening sight, indeed, and I closed my eyes to avoid seeing any more of it; but there was no need of that, for the writhing and struggling bodies of the two fell to the floor and so disappeared from sight.

Immediately afterward there was a tremendous crash. The roof had fallen in, and this was followed by an eruption of sparks and smoke and flame, accompanied by a violent roaring noise that sounded like the culmination of a storm. It was so loud that it aroused the pigeons on the place, and a great flock of them began circling around the burning building. Occasionally one more frightened than the rest would dart headlong into the flames, and it was curious to see the way it disappeared. There would be a fizz and a sputter, and the poor bird would be burnt harder than a crackling. I observed this and other commonplace things with unusual interest — an interest sharpened, perhaps, by the fact that there could be no hope for the two human beings on whom the roof had fallen.

Naturally, you will want to ask me a great many questions. I have asked them myself a thousand times, and I've tried to dream the answers to them while I sat dozing here in the sun, but when I dream about the affair at all, the fumes of burning flesh seem to fill my nostrils. Crooked-leg Jake insisted to the day of his death that the man who had driven our team sat in a chair in the corner of the dining-room, while the woman and the man were fighting, and seemed to be enjoying the spectacle. It may be so. At any rate none of us ever saw him again. As for the rest, you know just as much about it as I do.

MOM BI:

HER FRIENDS AND HER ENEMIES.

THE little town of Fairleigh, in South Carolina, was a noted place before the war, whatever it may be now. It had its atmosphere, as Judge Waynecroft used to say, and that atmosphere was one of distinction. It was a very quiet town, but there was something aristocratic, something exclusive, even in its repose. It was a rough wind that could disturb the stateliness of the live oaks with which the streets were lined, and it was indeed an inhospitable winter that could suppress the tendency of the roses to bloom.

Fairleigh made no public boast that it was not a commercial town, but there can be no doubt that it prided itself on the fact. Even the piney-woods crackers found a slow market there for the little "truck" they had to sell, for it was the custom of the people to get their supplies of all kinds from "the city." It was to "the city," indeed, that Fairleigh owed its prominence, and its inhabitants were duly mindful of that fact.

As late as 1854 there was no more insignificant village in South Carolina than Fairleigh; but in the summer of that year the fever plague flapped its yellow wings above Charleston, and the wealthier families sought safety in flight. Some went North and some went West; some went one way and some another; but the choice few, following the example of Judge Waynecroft, went no further than Fairleigh, which was far enough in the interior to be out of reach of the contagion.

They found the situation of the little village so convenient, and its climate so perfect, that they proceeded — still following the example of Judge Waynecroft — to build summer homes there; and in time Fairleigh became noted as a resort for the wealthiest and most refined people of Charleston.

Of this movement, as has been intimated, Judge Waynecroft was the pioneer; and for this and other reasons he was highly esteemed by the natives of Fairleigh. To their minds the Judge was an able and a public-spirited citizen, whom it was their pleasure to admire. In addition to this, he had a most charming household, in which simplicity lent grace to dignity.

There was one feature of Judge Waynecroft's household, however, which the natives of Fairleigh did not admire, and that was "Mom Bi." Perhaps they were justified in this. Mom Bi was a negro woman, who appeared to be somewhat past middle age, just how far past no one could guess. She was tall and gaunt, and her skin was black as jet. She walked rapidly, but with a sidewise motion, as if she had been overtaken with rheumatism or partial paralysis. Her left arm was bent and withered, and she carried it in front of her and across her body, as one would hold an infant. Her head-handkerchief was queerly tied. The folds of it stood straight up in the air, giving her the appearance of a black Amazon. This impression was heightened by the peculiar brightness of her eyes. They were not large eyes, but they shone like those of a wild animal that is not afraid of the hunter. Her nose was not flat, nor were her lips thick like those of the typical negro. Her whole appearance was aggressive. Moreover, her manner was abrupt, and her tongue sharp, especially when it was leveled at any of the natives of Fairleigh.

To do Mom Bi justice, her manner was abrupt and her tongue sharp even in her master's family, but there these matters were understood. Practically, she ruled the household, and though she quarreled from morning till night, and sometimes far into the night, everything she said was taken in a Pickwickian sense. She was an old family servant who not only had large privileges, but was defiantly anxious to take advantage of all of them.

Whatever effect slavery may have had on other negroes, or on negroes in general, it is certain that Mom Bi's spirit remained unbroken. Whoever crossed her in the least, white or black, old or young, got "a piece of her mind," and it was usually a very large piece. Naturally enough, under the circumstances, Mom Bi soon became as well known in Fairleigh and in all the region round about as any of the "quality people." To some, her characteristics were intensely irritating; while to others they were simply amusing; but to all she was a unique figure, superior in her methods and ideas to the common run of negroes.

Once, after having a quarrel with her mistress — a quarrel which was a one-sided affair, however — Mom Bi heard one of the house girls making an effort to follow her example. The girl was making some impertinent remarks to her mistress, when Mom Bi seized a dog-whip that was hanging in the hall, and used it with such effect that the pert young wench remembered it for many a long day.

This was Mom Bi's way. She was ready enough to quarrel with each and every member of her master's family, but she was ready to defend the entire household against any and all comers. Altogether she was a queer combination of tyrant and servant, of virago and "mammy." Yet her master and mistress appreciated and respected her, and the children loved her. Her strong individuality was not misunderstood by those who knew her best.

No one knew just how old she was, and no one knew her real name. Probably no one cared: but there was a tradition in the Waynecroft family that her name was Viola, and that it had been corrupted by the children into Bi — Mom Bi. As to her age, it is sufficient to say that she was the self-constituted repository of the oral history of three generations of the family. She was a young woman when her master's grandfather died in 1799. Good, bad or indifferent, Mom Bi knew all about the family; and there were passages in the careers of some of its members that she was fond of retailing to her master and mistress, especially when in a bad humor.

Insignificant as she was, Mom Bi made her influence felt in Fairleigh. She was respected in her master's family for her honesty and faithfulness, but outsiders shrank from her frank and fearless criticism. The "sandhillers" — the tackies — that marketed their poor little crops in and around the village, were the special objects of her aversion, and she lost no opportunity of harassing them. Whether these queer people regarded Mom Bi as a humorist of the grimmer sort, or whether they were indifferent to her opinions, it would be difficult to say, but it is certain that her remarks, no matter how personal or bitter, made little impression on them. The men would rub their thin beards, nudge each other and laugh silently, while the women would push their sunbonnets back and stare at her as if she were some rare curiosity on exhibition. At such times Mom Bi would laugh loudly and maliciously, and cry out in a shrill and an irritating tone: —

"De Lord know, I glad I nigger. Ef I ain't bin born black, dee ain't no tellin, what I mought bin born. I mought bin born lak some deze white folks what eat dirt un set in de chimerly-corner tell dee look lak dee bin smoke-dried. De Lord know what make Jesse Waynecroft fetch he famerly 'mongst folk lak deze."

This was mildness itself compared with some of Mom Bi's harangues later on, when the" sandhillers," urged by some of the energetic citizens of the village, were forming a military company to be offered to the Governor of Virginia for the defense of that State. This was in the summer of 1861. There was a great stir in the South. The martial spirit of the people had been aroused by the fiery eloquence of the political leaders, and the volunteers were mustering in every town and village. The "sandhillers" were not particularly enthusiastic — they had but vague ideas of the issues at stake — but the military business was something new to them, and therefore alluring. They volunteered readily if not cheerfully, and it was not long before there was a company of them mustering under the name of the Rifle Rangers — an attractive title to the ear if not to the understanding.

Mom Bi was very much interested in the maneuvers of the Rifle Rangers. She watched them with a scornful and a critical eye. Even in their uniforms, which were of the holiday pattern, their appearance was the reverse of soldierly. They were hollow-chested and round-shouldered, and exceedingly awkward in all their movements. Their maneuvers on the outskirts of the village, accompanied by the music of fife and drum, always drew a crowd of idlers, and among these interested spectators Mom Bi was usually to be found.

"Dee gwine fight," she would say to the Waynecroft children, in her loud and rasping voice. "Dee gwine kill folks right un left. Look at um! I done git skeer'd myse'f, dee look so 'vigrous. Ki! dee gwine eat dem Yankee up fer true. I sorry fer dem Yankee, un I skeer'd fer myse'f! When dee smell dem vittle what dem Yankee got, 't is good-by, Yankee! Look at um, honey! dee gwine fight fer rich folks' nigger."

The drilling and mustering went on, however, and Mom Bi was permitted to say what she pleased. Some laughed at her, others regarded her with something like superstitious awe, while a great many thought she was merely a harmless simpleton. Above all, she was Judge Waynecroft's family servant, and this fact was an ample apology in Fairleigh and its environs for anything that she might say.

The mustering of the "sandhillers" irritated Mom Bi; but when the family returned to Charleston in the winter, the preparations for war that she saw going on made a definite and profound impression on her. At night she would go into her mistress's room, sit on the hearth in a corner of the fire-place, and watch the fire in the grate. Nursing her withered arm, she would sit silent for an hour at a time, and when she did speak it seemed as if her tongue had lost something of its characteristic asperity.

"I think," said Mrs. Waynecroft, on one occasion, "that Mom Bi is getting religion."

"Well, she'll never get it any younger," the Judge replied.

Mom Bi, sitting in her corner, pretended

not to hear, but after a while she said: "Ef de Lord call me in de chu'ch, I gwine; ef he no call I no gwine — enty? I no yerry him call dis long time."

"Well," remarked the Judge, "something has cooled you off and toned you down, and I was in hopes you were in the mourners' seat."

"Huh!" exclaimed Mom Bi. "How come I gwine go in mourner seat? What I gwine do in dey?" Then pointing to a portrait of Gabriel Waynecroft hanging over the mantel, she cried out: "Wey he bin gone at?"

Gabriel was the eldest son, the hope and pride of the family. The Judge and his wife looked at each other.

"I think you know where he has gone," said Mrs. Waynecroft, gently. "He has gone to fight for his country."

"Huh!" the old woman grunted Then, after a pause, "Wey dem san'hillers bin gone at? Wey de country what dee fight fer?"

"Why, what are you talking about?" said Judge Waynecroft, who had been listening behind his newspaper. "This is their country too, and they have gone to fight for it."

"'Longside dat boy?" Mom Bi asked. Her voice rose as she pointed at Gabriel's picture.

"Why, certainly," said the Judge.

"*Pishou!*" exclaimed Mom Bi, with a hiss that was the very essence of scorn, contempt and unbelief. "Oona nee'n' tell me dat ting. I nuttin' but nigger fer true, but I know better dun dat. I bin nuss dat boy, un I know um troo un troo. Dat boy, 'e cut 'e t'roat fus' fo' 'e fight 'longside dem trash. When 'e be en tell-a you 'e gwine fight 'longside dem whut de Lord done fersooken dis long time?"

The Judge smiled, but Mrs. Waynecroft looked serious; Mom Bi rocked backward and forward, as if nursing her withered arm.

"Whut dem po' white trash gwine fight fer? Nuttin' 't all ain't bin tell me dat. Dee ain't bin had no nigger; dee ain't bin had no money; dee ain't bin had no lan'; dee ain't bin had nuttin' 't all. Un den 'pun top er dat, yer come folks fer tell me dat dat boy gwine fight 'longside dem creeturs."

Mom Bi laughed loudly, and shook her long finger at the portrait of young Gabriel Waynecroft. As a work of art the portrait was a failure, having been painted by an ambitious amateur; but, crude as it was, it showed a face of wonderful refinement. The features were as delicate as those of a woman, with the exception of the chin, which was full and firm. The eyes, large and lustrous, gazed from the canvas with a suggestion of both tenderness and fearlessness.

During the long and dreary days that followed — days of waiting, days of suffering and of sorrow — there were many changes in the Waynecroft household, but Mom Bi held her place. She remained as virile and as active as ever. If any change was noticeable it was that her temper was more uncertain and her voice shriller. All her talk was about the war; and as the contest wore on, with no perceptible advantage to the Confederates, she assumed the character and functions of a prophetess. Among the negroes, especially those who had never come in familiar contact with the whites, she was looked upon as a person to be feared and respected. Naturally, they argued that any black who talked to the white people as Mom Bi did must possess at least sufficient occult power to escape punishment.

Sometimes, in the pleasant weather, while walking with her mistress and the children on the battery at Charleston she would reach forth her hand and exclaim :

"Oona see dem wharfs? Dee gwine be fill wid Yankee ships! Dee gwine sail right stret up, un nuttin' 't all gwine stop um."

Then, turning to the town, she would say :

"Oona see dem street? Dee gwine fair swarm wid Yankee! Dee gwine march troo 'um, un nuttin' 't all gwine stop um. Oona see dem gang er nigger down dey? Dee gwine be free, un nuttin' 't all gwine stop um. Dee 'l be free, un ole Bi gwine be free. Ah, Lord! when de drum start fer beat, un de trumpet start fer blow, de white folks gwine los de nigger. Ki! I mos' yeddy dem now."

This was repeated, not once, but hundreds of times — in the house and on the streets, wherever Mom Bi went. At the market, while the venders were weighing out supplies for the Waynecroft household, Mom Bi would take advantage of the occasion to preach a sermon about the war and to utter prophecies about the freedom of the negroes. Her fearlessness was her best protection. Those who heard her had no doubt that she was a lunatic, and so she was allowed to come and go in peace, at a time when the great mass of the negroes were under the strictest surveillance. It made no difference to Mom Bi, however, whether one or a thousand eyes were watching her, or whether the whole world thought she was crazy. She was in earnest, and thus presented a spectacle that is rarer than a great many people are willing to admit.

The old woman went her way, affording amusement to some and to others food for thought; and the rest of the world went its way, especially that part of it that was watching events from rifle-pits and trenches. To those at home the years seemed to drag, though they went fast enough, no doubt, for those at the front. They went fast enough to mark some marvelous changes and developments. Hundreds of thousands of times, it happened that a gun fired in Virginia sorely wounded the hearts of a household far away.

On the Shenandoah, one night, a sharpshooter in blue heard the clatter of a horse's hoofs on the turnpike, and the jangling of sword, spurs and bit. As the horseman came into view in the moonlight, the sharpshooter leveled his rifle. There was a flash, a puff of smoke, and a report that broke into a hundred crackling echoes on the still night air. The horse that had been held so well in hand galloped wildly away with an empty saddle. The comrades of the cavalryman, who had been following him at a little distance, rushed forward at the report of the gun, and found their handsome young officer lying in the road, dead. They scoured the country for some distance around, but they saw nothing and heard nothing, and finally they lifted the dead soldier to a horse, and carried him back to their camp.

The sharpshooter had aimed only at the dashing young cavalryman, but his shot struck a father and a mother in Charleston, and an old negro woman who was supposed to be crazy; and the wounds that it made were grievous. The cavalryman was young Gabriel Waynecroft, and with the ending of his life the hope and expectations of the family seemed to be blotted out. He had been the darling of the household, the pride of his father, the joy of his mother, and the idol of Mom Bi. When the news of his death came, the grief of the household took the shape of consternation. It was terrible to behold. The mother was prostrated and the father crushed. Their sorrow was voiceless. Mom Bi went about wringing her hands and moaning and talking to herself day after day.

Once, Judge Waynecroft, passing through the hall in slippered feet, thought he heard voices in the sitting-room. In an aimless way, he glanced in the room, and the sight made him pause. Mom Bi was sitting in the middle of the room in a low chair, gazing at the portrait of Gabriel Waynecroft, and talking to it. She spoke in a soft and tender tone, in strange contrast to the usual rasping and irritating quality of her voice.

"Look at me, honey," she was saying; "look at you' ole nigger mammy! Whut make dee lef' you fer go way down, dey wey one folks kill turrer folks? Tell de ole nigger mammy dat, honey. Whaffer dee no lef' dem no 'count san'hillers fer do all de fightin'? Who gwine fer cry wun dee git kilt? Fightin' fer nigger! Whaffer you' daddy no sen' he niggers fer fight? De Lord know dee plenty un um. Nummine, honey! 'T aint gwine fer be long, 'fo' dee 'll all know whut de Lord know, un whut ole Bi know. Gi' um time, honey! des gi' um time!"

Judge Waynecroft turned away with a groan. To behold the bewildered grief of this old negro woman was to add a new pang to his own sorrow. Mom Bi paused, but did not turn her head. She heard her master pass down the hall with uncertain step, and then she heard the library door shut.

" 'Tis de gospel troot 'e bin yeddy me preachin'," she exclaimed. Then she turned again to the portrait and gazed at it steadily and in silence for a long while, rocking herself and nursing her withered arm.

When the body of Gabriel Waynecroft was brought home, Mom Bi kneeled on the floor at the foot of the coffin and stayed there, giving utterance to the wildest lamentations. Some friend or acquaintance of the family made an attempt to remove her.

"This will never do," he said kindly, but firmly. "You must get up and go away. The noise you are making distresses and disturbs the family."

Trembling with mingled grief and rage, Mom Bi turned upon the officious person.

"I ain't, I ain't, I ain't!" she almost shrieked. "I gwine fer stay right wey I is. Take you' han' fum off me, man! I bin cry on count dat chile mos' 'fo' he own mammy is. I bin nuss um, I bin worry wid um, I bin stay 'wake wid um wun ev'body wuz sleep, un I bin hol' um in my lap day un night, wun 'e sick un wun 'e well. I ain't gwine out! I ain't! I ain't!"

In fine, Mom Bi made a terrible scene, and the officious person who wanted to drive her out was glad to get out himself, which he was compelled to do in order to escape the clamor that he had unwittingly raised.

The death and burial of Gabriel Waynecroft was a gloomy episode in Mom Bi's experience, and it left its marks upon her. She lost none of her old-time vigor, but her temper became almost unbearable. She was surly, irritable and sometimes violent, especially toward the negroes on the place, who regarded her with a superstitious fear that would be difficult to explain or describe. Left to herself she did well enough. She loved to sit in the sun and talk to herself. The other negroes had a theory that she saw spirits and conversed with them; but they were welcome to their theories, so far as Mom Bi was concerned, provided they did n't pester her.

Meanwhile, Sherman's army was marching through Georgia to Savannah, and in Virginia Grant was arranging the plans of his last campaign. Savannah fell, and then came the information that Sherman's army was moving on Charleston. The city could be defended in only one direction: all its bristles pointed seaward; and the Confederate troops prepared to evacuate. All these movements were well known to the negroes, especially to Mom Bi, and she made use of her information to renew her prophecies. She stood in the porch of her master's house and watched the Confederates file by, greeting them occasionally with irritating comment.

"Hi! Wey you gwine? Whaffer you no stop fer tell folks good-by? Nummine! Dem Yankee buckra, dee gwine shaky you by de han'. Dee mek you hot fer true. Wey you no stop fer see de nigger come free?"

Most of Mom Bi's prophecies came true. Sherman marched northward, and then came Appomattox. One day, shortly after the surrender, Mom Bi appeared before Judge Waynecroft and his wife rigged out in her best clothes. She was rather more subdued than usual. She entered the room, and then stood still, looking first at one and then at the other.

"Well, Bi," said the Judge, kindly, "what can we do for you?"

"Nuttin' 't all. I gwine down dey at Sawanny, wey my daughter is bin live."

"Do you mean Maria?"

"My daughter 'Ria, w'at you bin sell to John Waynecroft. I gwine down dey wey she live at."

"Why, you are too old to be gadding about," said the Judge. "Why not stay here where you have a comfortable home?"

"I think you are very foolish to even dream of such a thing, Mom Bi. Maria is not able to take care of you."

"I gwine down dey wey my daughter bin live at," persisted Mom Bi. Then she looked at the portrait of Gabriel Waynecroft. The beautiful boyish face seemed to arouse her. Turning suddenly, she exclaimed:

"De Lord know I done bin fergive you-all fer sellin' 'Ria 'way fum me. De Lord know I is! Wun I bin see you set down un let dat chile go off fer git kill'" — Mom Bi pointed her long and quivering finger at Gabriel's portrait — "wun I see dis, I say 'hush up, nigger! don't bodder 'bout 'Ria.' De Lord know I done bin fergive you!'"

With this Mom Bi turned to the door and passed out.

"Won't you tell us good-by?" the Judge asked.

"I done bin fergive you," said Mom Bi.

"I think you might tell us good-by," said Mrs. Waynecroft, with tears in her eyes and voice.

"I done bin fergive you," was the answer.

This was in June. One morning months afterward Judge Waynecroft was informed by a policeman that a crazy old negro woman had been arrested in the cemetery.

"She is continually talking about Gabriel Waynecroft," said the officer, "and the Captain thought you might know something about her. She's got the temper of Old Harry," he continued, "and old and crippled as she is, she's as strong as a bull yearling."

It was Mom Bi, and she was carried to her old master's home. Little by little she told the story of her visit to Savannah. She found her daughter and her family in a most deplorable condition. The children had the small-pox, and finally Maria was seized with the disease. For lack of food and proper attention they all died, and Mom Bi found herself alone and friendless in a strange city. How she managed to make her way back home it is impossible to say, but she returned.

The Mom Bi who returned, however, was not the same Mom Bi that went away. Old age had overtaken her in Savannah. Her eyes were hollow, her face was pinched and shrunken, the flesh on her bones had shriveled, and her limbs shook as with the palsy. When she was helped into the house that had so long been her home she looked around at the furniture and the walls. Finally her eyes rested on the portrait of Gabriel Waynecroft. She smiled a little and then said feebly:

"I done bin come back. I bin come back fer stay; but I free, dough!"

In a little while she was freer still. She had passed beyond the reach of mortal care or pain; and, as in the old days, she went without bidding her friends good-by.

THE OLD BASCOM PLACE.

I.

One Saturday afternoon in the spring of 1876, as Farmer Joe-Bob Grissom was on his way to Hillsborough for the purpose of hearing the news and having an evening's chat with his town acquaintances, — as was his invariable custom at the close of the week, — he saw, as he passed the old Bascom Place, an old gentleman and a young lady walking slowly along the road. The old gentleman was tall and thin, and had silvery white hair. He wore a high-crowned, wide-brimmed felt hat, and his clothes, though neat, were too glossy to be new. The young lady was just developing into womanhood. She had a striking face and figure. Her eyes were large and brilliantly black; her hair, escaping from under her straw hat with its scarlet ribbons, fell in dusky masses to her waist.

The two walked slowly, and occasionally they paused while the old gentleman pointed in various directions with his cane, as though impressing on the mind of his companion the whereabouts of certain interesting landmarks. They were followed at a little distance by a negro, who carried across his arm a light wrap which seemed to be a part of the outfit of the young lady.

As Farmer Joe-Bob Grissom passed the two, he bowed and tipped his hat by way of salutation. The old gentleman raised his hat and bowed with great courtliness, and the young lady nodded her head and smiled pleasantly at him. Farmer Joe-Bob was old enough to be grizzly, but the smile stirred him. It seemed to be a direct challenge to his memory. Where had he seen the young lady before? Where had he met the old gentleman? He was puzzled to such an extent that he paid no attention to the negro man, who touched his hat and bowed politely as the farmer passed — a fact that made the negro wonder a little; for day in and out he had known Mr. Joe-Bob Grissom nearly forty years, and never before had that worthy citizen failed to respond with a cordial "Howdy" when the negro took off his hat.

Farmer Joe-Bob Grissom walked on towards town, which was not far, and the old gentleman and the young lady walked slowly along the hedge of Cherokee roses that ran around the old Bascom Place, while the negro followed at a respectful distance. Once they paused, and the old gentleman rubbed his eyes with a hand that trembled a little.

"Why, darling!" he exclaimed in a tone of mingled grief and astonishment, "they have cut it down."

"Cut what down, father?"

"Why, the weeping-willow. Don't you remember it, daughter? It stood in the middle of the field yonder. It was a noble tree. Well, well, well! What next, I wonder?"

"I do not remember it, father; I have so much to" —

"Yes, yes," the old gentleman interrupted. "Of course you couldn't remember. The place has been so changed that I seem to have forgotten it myself. It has been turned topsy-turvy; it has been ruined — ruined!"

He leaned on his cane, and with quivering lips and moist eyes looked through the green perspective of the park, and over the fertile fields and meadows.

"Ruined!" exclaimed the young lady. "How can you say so, father? I never saw a more beautiful place. It would make a lovely picture."

"And they have ruined the house, too. The whole roof has been changed." The old man pulled his hat down over his eyes, his hand trembling more than ever. "Let us turn back, Mildred," he said after a while. "The sight of all this frets and worries me more than I thought it would."

"They say," said the daughter, "that the gentleman who owns the place has made a good deal of money."

"Yes," replied the father, "I suppose so — I suppose so. Yes, so I have heard. A great many people are making money now who never made it before — a great many."

"I wish they would tell us the secret," said the young lady, laughing a little.

"There is no secret about it," said the old gentleman; "none whatever. To make money you must be mean and niggardly yourself, and then employ others to be mean and niggardly for you."

"Oh, it is not always so, father," the young girl exclaimed.

"It *was* not always so, my daughter.

There *was* a time when one could make money and remain a gentleman; but that was many years ago."

The young lady was apparently not anxious to continue the argument, for she lightly turned the conversation into a more agreeable channel; and so the two, still followed by the negro, made their way through the shaded streets of the town.

That evening, when Mr. Joe-Bob Grissom, after making some little purchases about town, went to the hotel, which he persisted in calling a tavern, he found Major Jimmy Bass engaged in a hot political discussion with a crowd which included a number of the townspeople, as well as a sprinkling of commercial travelers. Major Jimmy was one of the ancient and venerable landmarks of that region. He had once been an active politician, and had been engaged in political discussion for forty years or more. Old and fat as he was, he knew how to talk, and nothing pleased him more than to get hold of a stranger when a crowd of sympathetic fellow-citizens, young and old, was present to applaud the points he made.

Whenever Mr. Joe-Bob Grissom appeared in the veranda of the hotel he made it a point to shake hands with every person present, friend and stranger alike. His politeness was a trifle elaborate, but it was genuine.

"Why, howdy, Joe-Bob, howdy!" exclaimed Major Bass with effusion. "You seem to turn up at the right time, like the spangled man in the circus. I'm glad you've come, an' ef I'd 'a' had my way you'd 'a' come sooner, bekaze you're jest a little too late fer to see me slap the argyments onto some of these here travelin' drummers. They are gone now," the major continued, with a sweeping gesture of his right arm. "They are gone, but I wisht mightily you'd 'a' been here. New things is mortal nice, I know; but when these new-issue chaps set up to out-talk men that's old enough to be their grand-daddy, it does me a sight of good fer to see 'em took down a peg er two."

As soon as he could get in a word edgewise, farmer Joe-Bob Grissom attempted to turn the conversation in a direction calculated to satisfy his curiosity.

"Major," he said in his deliberate way, "what's this I see out yonder at the old Bascom Place?"

"The Lord only knows, Joe-Bob. What might be the complexion, er yet the character, of it?"

"Well," said Mr. Grissom, "as I was makin' to'rds town a little while ago, I seen some folks that don't look like they b'long 'roun' here. One of 'em was a old man, an' t' other one was a young gal, an' a nigger man was a-follerin' of 'em up — an', ef I make no mistakes, the nigger man was your old Jess. I did n't look close at the nigger, but arter I 'd passed him it come to me that it wa' n't nobody on the topside of the roun' worl' but Jess."

"Why, bless your life an' soul!" exclaimed Major Bass, giving farmer Joe-Bob a neighborly nudge, "don't you know who them folks was? Well, well! Where 's your mind? Why, that was old Briscoe Bascom an' his daughter."

"I say it!" exclaimed farmer Joe-Bob, hitching his chair closer to the major.

"Yes, sir," said the major, "that 's who it was. Why, where on earth have you been? The old Judge drapped in on the town some weeks ago, an' he 's been here ever sence. He 's been here long enough for the gal to make up a school. Lord,

Lord! What a big swing the world's in! High on one side, high on t' other, an' the old cat a-dyin, in the middle! Why, bless your heart, Joe-Bob! I've seed the time when ef old Judge Briscoe Bascom jest so much as bowed to me I'd feel proud fer a week. An' now look at 'im! Ef I knowed I'd be took off wi' the dropsy the nex' minute, I would n't swap places wi' the poor old creetur."

"But what is old Jess a-doin' doggin' 'long arter 'em that a-way?" inquired Mr. Grissom, knitting his shaggy eyebrows.

"That's what pesters me," exclaimed the major. "Ef niggers was ree-sponsible fer what they done, it would be wuss than what it is. Now you take Jesse: you need n't tell me that nigger ain't got sense; yit what does he do? You seen 'im wi' your own eyes. Why, sir," continued the major, growing more emphatic, "I bought that nigger from Judge Bascom's cousin when he wa' n't nothin' but a youngster, an' I took him home an' raised him up right in the house, — yes, sir, right in the house, — an' he's been a-hangin' 'roun' me off an' on, gittin' his vittles, his clozes, an' his lodgin'. Yit, look at him now! I wisht I may die dead ef that nigger did n't hitch onto old Judge Bascom the minute he landed in town. Yes, sir! I'm a-tellin' you no lie. It's a clean, naked fact. That nigger quit me an' went an' took up wi' the old judge."

"Well," said Mr. Grissom, stroking his unshorn face, "you know what the sayin' is: Niggers 'll be niggers even ef you whitewash 'em twice a week."

"Yes," remarked the major thoughtfully; "I hope to goodness they've got souls, but I misdoubt it. Lord, yes, I misdoubt it mightily."

II.

As Major Jimmy Bass used to say, the years cut many queer capers as they go by. The major in his own proper person had not only witnessed, but had been the victim, of these queer capers. Hillsborough was a very small place indeed, and, for that very reason perhaps, it was more sensitive to changes in the way of progress and decay than many larger and more ambitious towns.

However this may have been, it is certain that the town, assisted by the major, had noted the queer capers the years had cut in the neighborhood of the old Bascom Place. This attitude on the part of Hillsborough — including, of course, Major Jimmy Bass — may be accounted for partly by the fact that the old place had once been the pride and delight of the town, and partly by the fact that the provincial eye and mind are nervously alert to whatever happens within range of their observation.

Before and during the war the Bascom Place was part and parcel of a magnificent estate. The domain was so extensive and so well managed that it was noted far and wide. Its boundary lines inclosed more than four thousand acres of forests and cultivated fields. This immense body of land was known as the old Bascom Place.

Bolling Bascom, its first owner, went to Georgia not long after the close of the Revolution, with a large number of Virginians who proposed to establish a colony in what was then the far South. The colony settled in Wilkes County; but Bolling Bascom, more adventurous than the rest, pushed on into middle Georgia, crossed the Oconee, and built him a home, and such was his taste, his energy, and his thrift, that the results thereof may be seen and admired in Hillsborough to this day.

But the man, like so many of his fellow-citizens then and thereafter, was land-hungry, He bought and bought until he had aquired the immense domain, which, by some special interposition of fate or circumstance, is still intact. Meantime he had built him a house which was in keeping with the extent and richness of his landed possessions. It was planned in the old colonial style, but its massive proportions were relieved by the tall red chimneys and the long and gracefully fashioned colonnade that gave both strength and beauty to the spacious piazza which ran, and still runs, the whole length of the house.

When Bolling Bascom died, in 1830, aged seventy years, as the faded inscription on the storm-beaten tablet in the churchyard shows, he left his son, Briscoe Bascom, to own and manage the vast estate. This son was thirty years old, and it was said of him that he inherited the gentle qualities of his mother rather than the fiery energy and ambition of his father.

Bolling Bascom was neither vicious nor reckless, but he was a thorough man of the world. He was, in short, a typical Virginian gentleman, who for his own purposes had settled in Georgia,

Whatever the cause of his emigration, it is certain that Georgia gained a good citizen. It was said of him that he was a little too fond of a fiddle, but with all his faults — with all his love for horse-racing and fox-hunting — he found time to be kind to his neighbors, generous to his friends, and the active leader of every movement calculated to benefit the State or the people; and it may be remarked in passing, that he also found time to look after his own affairs.

Naturally, he was prominent in politics. He represented his county in the legislature, was at one time a candidate for governor, and was altogether a man who had the love and the confidence of his neighbors. He gave his son the benefit of the best education the country afforded, and made the tour of Europe with him, going over the ground that he himself had gone over in his young days.

But his European trip, undertaken when he was an old man, was too much for him. He was seized with an illness on his return voyage, and, although he lived long enough to reach home, he never recovered. In a few years his wife died; and his son, with little or no experience in such matters, —

since his time had been taken up by the schools and colleges, — was left to manage the estate as best he could.

It was the desire of Bolling Bascom that his son should study law and make that profession a stepping-stone to a political career. He had been ambitious himself, and he hoped his son would also be ambitious. Besides, was not politics the most respectable of all the professions? This was certainly the view in Bolling Bascom's day and time, and much might be said to support it. Of all the professions, politics opened up the one career best calculated to tickle the fancy of the rich young men.

To govern, to control, to make laws, to look after the welfare of the people, to make great speeches, to become statesmen — these were the ideas that filled the minds of ambitious men in Bolling Bascom's time, and for years thereafter. And why not? There were the examples of Jefferson, Madison, Monroe, Randolph, Hamilton, Webster, Calhoun, and the Adamses of Massachusetts. What better could a young man do than to follow in the footsteps of these illustrious citizens?

It may be supposed, therefore, that Bolling Bascom had mapped out a tremendous career for his son and heir. No doubt, as he sat dozing on his piazza in the long summer afternoons near the close of his life, he fancied he could hear the voice of his boy in the halls of legislation, or hear the wild shouts of the multitudes that greeted his efforts on the stump in the heat and fury of a campaign. But it was not to be. The stormy politics of that period had no charms for Briscoe Bascom. He was a student, and he preferred his book to the companionship of the crowd.

He possessed both courage and sociability in the highest degree, but he was naturally indolent, and he was proud — too indolent to find pleasure in the whirling confusion of active politics, and too proud to go about his county or his State in the attitude of soliciting the suffrages of his fellow-citizens. That he would have made his mark in politics is certain, for he made it at the bar, where success is much more dearly bought. He finally became judge of the superior court, at a time when the judges of the circuit courts met annually and formed a court of appeals. His decisions in this appellate court attracted attention all over the country, and are still referred to in the legal literature of to-day as models of their kind.

And yet all that Briscoe Bascom accomplished at the bar and on the bench was the result of intuition rather than of industry. Indolence sat enthroned in his nature, patient but vigilant. When he retired from the bench, he gave up the law altogether. He might have reclaimed his large practice, but he preferred the ease and quiet of his home.

He was an old man before he married — old enough, that is to say, to marry a woman many years his junior. His wife had been reared in an atmosphere of extravagance; and although she was a young woman of gentle breeding and of the best intentions, it is certain that she did not go to the Bascom Place as its mistress for the purpose of stinting or economizing. She simply gave no thought to the future. But she was so bright and beautiful, so gentle and unaffected in speech and manner, so gracious and so winsome in all directions, that it seemed nothing more than natural and right that her every whim and wish should be gratified.

Judge Bascom was indulgent and more

than indulgent. He applauded his wife's extravagance and followed her example. Before many years he began to reap some of the fruits thereof, and they were exceeding bitter to the taste. The longest purse that ever was made has a bottom to it, unless, indeed, it be lined with Franklin's maxims.

The Judge was forty-eight years old when he married, and even before the beginning of the war he found his financial affairs in an uncomfortable condition. The Bascom Place was intact, but the pocket-book of its master was in a state bordering on collapse.

The slow but sure approach to the inevitable need not be described here. It is familiar to all people in all lands and times. In the case of Judge Bascom, however, the war was in the nature of a breathing-spell. It brought with it an era of extravagance that overshadowed everything that had been dreamed of theretofore. During the first two years there was money enough for everybody and to spare. It was manufactured in Richmond in great stacks. General Robert Toombs, who was an interested observer, has aptly described the facility with which the Confederacy supplied itself with money. "A dozen negroes," said he, "printed money on the hand-presses all day to supply the government, and then they worked until nine o'clock at night printing money enough to pay themselves off."

Under these circumstances, Judge Bascom and his charming wife could be as extravagant or as economical as they pleased without attracting the attention of their neighbors or their creditors. Nobody had time to think or care about such small matters. The war-fever was at its height, and nothing else occupied the attention of the people. The situation was so favorable, indeed, that Judge Bascom began to redeem his fortune — in Confederate money. He had land enough and negroes a plenty, and so he saved his money by storing it away; and he was so successful in this business that it is said that when the war closed he had a wagon-load of Confederate notes and shinplaster packed in trunks and chests.

The crash came when General Sherman went marching through Hillsborough. The Bascom Place, being the largest and the richest plantation in that neighborhood, suffered the worst. Every horse, every mule, every living thing with hide and hoof, was driven off by the Federals; and a majority

of the negroes went along with the army.
It was often said of Judge Bascom that " he
had so many negroes he did n't know them
when he met them in the big road;" and
this was probably true. His negroes knew
him, and knew that he was a kind master in
many respects, but they had no personal
affection for him. They were such strangers
to the Judge that they never felt justified in
complaining to him even when the overseers
ill-treated them. Consequently, when Sherman went marching along, the great majority of them bundled up their little effects
and followed after the army. They had
nothing to bind them to the old place. The
house-servants, and a few negroes in whom
the Judge took a personal interest, remained,
but all the rest went away.

Then, in a few months, came the news of
the surrender, bringing with it a species of
paralysis or stupefaction from which the
people were long in recovering — so long,
indeed, that some of them died in despair,
while others lingered on the stage, watching,
with dim eyes and trembling limbs, half-
hopefully and half-fretfully, the representatives of a new generation trying to build up
the waste places. There was nothing left

for Judge Bascom to do but to take his place among the spectators. He would have returned to his law-practice, but the people had well-nigh forgotten that he had ever been a lawyer; moreover, the sheriffs were busier in those days than the lawyers. He had the incentive, — for the poverty of those days was pinching, — but he lacked the energy and the strength necessary to begin life anew. He and hundreds like him were practically helpless. Ordinarily experience is easily learned when necessity is the teacher, but it was too late for necessity to teach Judge Bascom anything. During all his life he had never known what want was. He had never had occasion to acquire tact, business judgment, or economy. Inheriting a vast estate, he had no need to practice thrift or become familiar with the shifty methods whereby business men fight their way through the world. Of all such matters he was entirely ignorant.

To add to his anxiety, a girl had been born to him late in life, his first and only child. In his confusion and perplexity he was prepared to regard the little stranger as merely a new and dreadful responsibility, but it was not long before his daughter was a source of great comfort to him. Yet, as the negroes said, she was not a "luck-child;" and bad as the Judge's financial condition was, it grew steadily worse.

Briefly, the world had drifted past him and his contemporaries and left them stranded. Under the circumstances, what was he to do? It is true he had a magnificent plantation, but this merely added to his poverty. Negro labor was demoralized, and the overseer class had practically disappeared. He would have sold a part of his landed estate; indeed, so pressing were his needs that he would have sold everything except the house which his father had built, and where he himself was born, — that he would not have parted with for all the riches in the world, — but there was nobody to buy. The Judge's neighbors and his friends, with the exception of those who had accustomed themselves to seizing all contingencies by the throat and wresting tribute from them, were in as severe a strait as he was; and to make matters worse, the political affairs of the State were in the most appalling condition. It was the period of reconstruction — a scheme that paralyzed all whom it failed to corrupt.

Finally the Judge's wife took matters into her own hand. She had relatives in Atlanta, and she prevailed on him to go to that lively and picturesque town. He closed his house, being unable to rent it, and became a citizen of the thrifty city. He found himself in a new atmosphere. The north Georgia crackers, the east Tennesseeans, — having dropped their "you-uns" and "we-uns," — and the Yankees had joined hands in building up and pushing Atlanta forward. Business was more important than politics; and the rush and whirl of men and things were enough to make a mere spectator dizzy. Judge Bascom found himself more helpless than ever; but through the influence of his wife's brother he was appointed to a small clerkship in one of the State departments, and — "Humiliation of humiliations!" his friends exclaimed — he promptly accepted it, and became a part of what was known as the "carpet-bag" government. The appointment was in the nature of a godsend, but the Judge found himself ostracized. His friends and acquaintances refused to return his salutation as he met them on the street. To a proud and sensitive man this was the bitterness of death, but Judge Bascom stuck to his desk and made no complaint.

By some means or other, no doubt through the influence of Mrs. Bascom, the Judge's brother-in-law, a thrifty and not over-scrupulous man, obtained a power of attorney, and sold the Bascom Place, house and all, to a gentleman from western New York who was anxious to settle in middle Georgia. Just how much of the purchase-money went into the Judge's hands it is impossible to say, but it is known that he fell into a terrible rage when he was told that the house had been sold along with the place. He denounce the sale as a swindle, and declared that as he had been born in the house he would die there, and not all the powers of earth could prevent him.

But the money that he received was a substantial thing as far as it went. Gradually he found himself surrounded by various comforts that he had sadly missed, and in time he became somewhat reconciled to the sale, though he never gave up the idea that he would buy the old place back and live there again. The idea haunted him day and night.

After the downfall of the carpet-bag administration a better feeling took possession of the people and politicians, and it was not long before Judge Bascom found congenial work in codifying the laws of the State, which had been in a somewhat confused and tangled condition since the war. Meanwhile his daughter Mildred was growing up, developing remarkable beauty as well as strength of mind. At a very early age she began to "take the responsibility," as the Judge put it, of managing the household affairs, and she continued to manage them even while going to school. At school she won the hearts of teachers and pupils, not less by her aptitude in her books than by her beauty and engaging manners.

But in spite of the young girl's management — in spite of the example she set by her economy — the Judge and his wife continued to grow poorer and poorer. Neither of them knew the value of a dollar, and the money that had been received from the sale of the Bascom Place was finally exhausted. About this time Mrs. Bascom died, and the Judge was so prostrated by his bereavement that it was months before he recovered. When he did recover he had lost all interest in his work of codification, but it was so nearly completed and was so admirably done that the legislature voted him extra pay. This modest sum the daughter took charge of, and when her father was well enough she proposed that they return to Hillsborough, where they could take a small house, and where she could give music lessons and teach a primary school. It need not be said that the Judge gave an eager assent to the proposition.

III.

As Mr. Joe-Bob Grissom passed the Bascom Place on his way home, after gathering from Major Jimmy Bass all the news and gossip of the town, he heard Mr. Francis Underwood, the owner of the Place, walking up and down the piazza, singing. Mr. Underwood appeard to be in a cheerful mood, and he had a right to be. He was young, — not more than thirty, — full of life, and the world was going on very well with him. Mr. Grissom paused a moment and listened; then he made up his mind to go in and have a chat with the young man. He opened the gate and went up the avenue under the cedars and Lombardy poplars. A little distance from the house he was stopped by a large mastiff. The great dog made no attempt to attack him, but majestically barred the way.

"Squire," yelled Joe-Bob, "ef you'll call off your dog, I'll turn right 'roun' an' go home an' never bother you no more."

"Is that you, Joe-Bob?" exclaimed Mr. Underwood. "Well, come right on. The dog won't trouble you."

The dog thereupon turned around and went up the avenue to the house and into the porch, where he stretched himself out at full length, Joe-Bob following along at a discreet distance.

"Come in," said Underwood heartily; "I'm glad to see you. Take this large rocking-chair; you will find it more comfortable than the smaller one."

Mr. Grissom sat down and looked cautiously around to see where the dog was.

"I did come, Squire," he said, "to see you on some kinder business, but that dratted dog has done skeered it clean out 'n me."

"Prince is a faithful watcher," said Underwood, "but he never troubles any one who is coming straight to the house. Do you, old fellow?" The dog rapped an answer on the floor with his tail.

"Well," said Joe-Bob, "I'd as lief be tore up into giblets, mighty nigh, as to have my sev'm senses skeered out'n me. What I'm afeared of now," he went on, "is that that dog will jump over the fence some day an' ketch old Judge Bascome whilst he's a-pirootin' 'roun' here a-lookin' at the old Place. An' ef he don't ketch the Judge, it's more 'n likely he 'll ketch the Judge's gal. I seen both of 'em this very evenin' whilst I was a-goin' down town."

"Was that the Judge?" exclaimed young Mr. Underwood, with some show of interest; "and was the lady his daughter? I heard they had returned."

"That was jest percisely who it was," said Joe-Bob with emphasis. "It wa' n't nobody else under the shinin' sun."

"Well," said Mr. Underwood, "I have seen them walking by several times. It is natural they should be interested in the Place. The old gentleman was born here?"

"Yes," said Joe-Bob, "an' the gal too. They tell me," he went on, "that the old Judge an' his gal have seed a many ups an' downs. I reckon they er boun' fer to feel lonesome when they come by an' look at the prop'ty that use' to be theirn. I hear tell that the old Judge is gwine to try an' see ef he can't git it back."

Francis Underwood said nothing, but sat gazing out into the moonlight as if in deep thought.

"I thinks, says I," continued Joe-Bob, "that the old Judge 'll have to be lots pearter 'n he looks to be ef he gits ahead of Squire Underwood."

The "Squire" continued to gaze reflectively down the dim perspective of cedars and Lombardy poplars. Finally he said:—

"Have a cigar, old man. These are good ones."

Joe-Bob took the cigar and lighted it, handling it very gingerly.

"I ain't a denyin' but what they are good, Squire, but somehow er nuther me an' these here fine seegyars don't gee," said Joe-Bob, as he puffed away. "They 're purty toler'ble nice, but jest about the time I git in the notion of smokin' they 're done burnted up, an' then ef you ain't got sev'm or eight more, it makes you feel mighty lonesome. Now I 'll smoke this 'n', an' it 'll sorter put my teeth on edge fer my pipe, an' when I git home I 'll set up an' have a right nice time."

THE OLD BASCOM PLACE.

"And so you think," said Underwood, speaking as if he had not heard Joe-Bob's remarks about the cigar — "and so you think Judge Bascom has come to buy the old Place."

"No, no!" said Joe-Bob, with a quick deprecatory gesture. "Oh, no, Squire! not by no means! No, no! I never said them words. What I did say was that it's been talked up an' down that the old Judge is a-gwine to try to git his prop'ty back. That's what old Major Jimmy Bass said he heard, an' I thinks, says I, he'll have to be monst'us peart ef he gits ahead of Squire Underwood. That's what I said to myself, an' then I ast old Major Jimmy, says I, what the Judge would do wi' the prop'ty arter he got it, an' Major Jimmy, he ups an' says, says he, that the old Judge would sell it back to Frank Underwood, says he."

The young man threw back his head and laughed heartily, not less at the comical earnestness of Joe-Bob Grissom than at the gossip of Major Jimmy Bass.

"It seems, then, that we are going to have lively times around here," said Underwood, by way of comment.

"Yes, siree," exclaimed Joe-Bob; "that's

what Major Jimmy Bass allowed. Do you reckon, Squire," he continued, lowering his voice as though the matter was one to be approached cautiously, "do you reckon, Squire, they could slip in on you an' trip you up wi' one of 'em writs of arousement or one of 'em bills of injectment?"

"Not unless they catch me asleep," replied Underwood, still laughing. "We get up very early in the morning on this Place."

"Well," said Joe-Bob Grissom, "I ain't much of a lawyer myself, an' so I thought I'd jest drap in an' tell you the kind of talk what they 've been a-rumorin' 'roun'. But I'll tell you what you kin do, Squire. Ef the wust comes to the wust, you kin make the old Judge an' the gal take you along wi' the Place. Now them would be my politics."

With that Joe-Bob gave young Underwood a nudge in the short ribs, and chuckled to such an extent that he nearly strangled himself with cigar smoke.

"I think I would have the best of the bargain," said the young man.

"Now you would! you reely would!" exclaimed Joe-Bob in all seriousness. "I can't tell you the time when I ever seed a likelier gal than that one wi' the Judge this evenin'. As we say down here in Georgia, she's the top of the pot an' the pot a-b'ilin'. I tell you that right pine-blank."

After a little, Mr. Grissom rose to go. When Mr. Underwood urged him to sit longer, he pointed to the sword and belt of Orion hanging low in the southwest.

"The ell an' yard are a-makin' the'r disappearance," he said; "an' ef I stay out much longer, my old 'oman 'll think I've been a-settin' up by a jug somewheres. Now ef you'll jest hold your dog, Squire, I'll go out as peaceful as a lamb."

"Why, I was just going to propose to send him down to the big gate with you," said young Underwood. "He'll see you safely out."

"No, no, Squire!" exclaimed Joe-Bob, holding up both hands. "Now don't do the like of that. I don't like too much perliteness in folks, an' I know right well I could n't abide it in a dog. No, Squire; jest hold on to the creetur' wi' both hands, an' I'll find my way out. Jest ketch him by the forefoot. I've heard tell before now that ef you'll hold a dog by his forefoot he can't git loose, an' nuther kin he bite you."

Long after Mr. Joe-Bob Grissom had gone home young Francis Underwood sat in his piazza smoking and thinking. He had a good deal to think about, too, for he was perhaps the busiest and the thriftiest person that Hillsborough had ever seen. He had a dairy farm stocked with the choicest strains of Jersey cattle, and he shipped hundreds of pounds of golden butter all over the country every week in the year; he bred Percheron horses for farm-work and trotting-horses for the road; he had a flourishing farm on which he raised, in addition to his own supplies, a hundred or more bales of cotton every year; he had a steam saw-mill and cotton-gin; he was a contractor and builder; and he was also an active partner in the largest store in Hillsborough. Moreover he took a lively interest in the affairs of the town. His energy and his progressive ideas seemed to be contagious, for in a few years the sleepy old town had made tremendous strides, and everything appeared to move forward with an air of business — such is the force of a genial and robust example.

There is no doubt that young Underwood was somewhat coolly received when he first made his appearance in Hillsborough. He was a New Yorker and therefore a Yankee; and some of the older people, who were still grieving over the dire results of the war, as old people have a right to do, made no concealment of their prejudices. Their grief was too bitter to be lightly disposed of. Perhaps the young man appreciated this fact, for his sympathies were wonderfully quick and true. At any rate, he carried himself as buoyantly and as genially in the face of prejudice as he did afterwards in the face of friendship.

The truth is, prejudice could not stand before him. He had that magnetic personality which is a more precious possession than fame or fortune. There was something attractive even in his restless energy; he had that heartiness of manner and graciousness of disposition that are so rare among men; and, withal, a spirit of independence that charmed the sturdy-minded people with whom he cast his lot. It was not long before the younger generation began to seek Mr. Underwood out, and after this the social ice, so to speak, thawed quickly.

In short, young Underwood, by reason of a strong and an attractive individuality, became a very prominent citizen of Hillsborough. He found time, in the midst of his own business enterprises, to look after the interests of the town and the county. One of his first movements was to organize an agricultural society which held its meeting four times a year in different parts of the county. It was purely a local and native suggestion, however, that made it incumbent on the people of the neighborhood where the Society met to grace the occasion with a feast in the shape of a barbecue. The first result of the agricultural society — which still exists, and which has had a wonderful influence on the farmers of middle Georgia — was a county fair, of which Mr. Underwood was the leading spirit. It may be said, indeed, that his energy and his money made the fair possible. And it was a success. Young Underwood had not only canvassed the county, but he had "worked it up in the newspapers," as the phrase goes, and it tickled the older citizens immensely to see the dailies in the big cities of Atlanta, Macon, and Savannah going into rhetorical raptures over their fair.

As a matter of fact, Francis Underwood, charged with the fiery energy of a modern

American, found it a much easier matter to establish himself in the good graces of the people of Hillsborough and the surrounding country than did Judge Bascom when he returned to his old home with his lovely daughter. Politically speaking, he had committed the unpardonable sin when he accepted office under what was known as the carpet-bag government. It was an easy matter — thus the argument ran — to forgive and respect an enemy, but it was hardly possible to forgive a man who had proved false to his people and all their traditions — who had, in fact, "sold his birthright for a mess of pottage," to quote the luminous language employed by Colonel Bolivar Blasingame in discussing the return of Judge Bascom. It is due to Colonel Blasingame to say that he did not allude to the sale of the Bascom Place, but to the fact that Judge Bascom had drawn a salary from the State treasury while the Republicans were in power in Georgia.

This was pretty much the temper of the older people of Hillsborough even in 1876. They had no bitter prejudices against the old Judge; they were even tolerant and kindly; but they made it plain to him that he was regarded in a new light, and from a new standpoint. He was made to feel that his old place among them must remain vacant; that the old intimacies were not to be renewed. But this was the price that Judge Bascom was willing to pay for the privilege of spending his last days within sight of the old homestead. He made no complaints, nor did he signify by word or sign, even to his daughter, that everything was not as it used to be.

As for the daughter, she was in blissful ignorance of the situation. She was a stranger among strangers, and so was not affected by the lack of sociability on the part of the townspeople — if, indeed, there was any lack so far as she was concerned. The privations she endured in common with her father were not only sufficient to correct all notions of vanity or self-conceit, but they had given her a large experience of life; they had broadened her views and enlarged her sympathies, so that with no sacrifice of the qualities of womanly modesty and gentleness she had grown to be self-reliant. She attracted all who came within range of her sweet influence, and it was not long before she had broken down all the barriers that prejudice against her father might have placed in her way. She established a primary school, and what with her duties there and with her music-class she soon had as much as she could do, and her income from these sources was sufficient to support herself and her father in a modest way; but it was not sufficient to carry out her father's plans, and this fact distressed her no little.

Sometimes Judge Bascom, sitting in the narrow veranda of the little house they occupied, would suddenly arouse himself, as if from a doze, and exclaim: —

"We must save money, daughter; we must save money and buy the old Place back. It is ours. We must have it; we must save money." And sometimes, in the middle of the night, he would go to his daughter's bedside, stroke her hair, and say in a whisper: —

"We are not saving enough money, daughter; we must save more. We must buy the old Place back. We must save it from ruin."

IV.

There was one individual in Hillsborough who did not give the cold shoulder to

Judge Bascom on his return, and that was the negro Jesse, who had been bought by Major Jimmy Bass some years before the war from Merriwether Bascom, a cousin of the Judge. Jesse made no outward demonstration of welcome; he was more practical than that. He merely went to his old master with whom he had been living since he became free, and told him that he was going to find employment elsewhere.

"Why, what in the nation!" exclaimed Major Bass. "Why, what's the matter, Jess?"

The very idea was preposterous. In the Bass household the negro was almost indispensable. He was in the nature of a piece of furniture that holds its own against all fashions and fills a place that nothing else can fill.

"Dey ain't nothin' 't all de matter, Marse Maje. I des took it in my min', like, dat I'd go off some'r's roun' town en set up fer myse'f," said Jesse, scratching his head in a dubious way. He felt very uncomfortable.

"Has anybody hurt your feelin's, Jess?"

"No, suh! Lord, no, suh, dat dey ain't!" exclaimed Jesse, with the emphasis of astonishment. "Nobody ain't pester me."

"Ain't your Miss Sarah been rushin' you roun' too lively fer to suit your notions?"

"No, suh."

"Ain't she been a-quarrelin' after you about your work?"

"No, Marse Maje; she ain't say a word."

"Well, then, Jess, what in the name of common sense are you gwine off fer?" The major wanted to argue the matter.

"I got it in my min', Marse Maje, but I dunno ez I kin git it out straight." Jesse leaned his cane against the house, and placed his hat on the steps, as if preparing for a lengthy and elaborate explanation. "Now den, hit look dis way ter me, des like I'm gwine ter tell you. I ain't nothin' but a nigger, I know dat mighty well, en nobody don't hafter tell me. I'm a nigger, en you a white man. You're a-settin' up dar in de peazzer, en I'm a-stan'in' down yer on de groun'. I been wid you a long time; you treat me well, you gimme plenty vittles, en you pay me up when you got de money, en I hustle roun' en do de bes' I kin in de house en in de gyarden. Dat de way it been gwine on; bofe un us feel like it all sati'factual. Bimeby it come over me dat maybe I kin do mo' work dan what I been a-doin' en git mo' money. Hit work roun' in my min' dat I better be layin' up somepin' n'er fer de ole 'oman en de chillun."

"Well!" exclaimed Major Bass with a snort. It was all he could say.

"En den ag'in," Jesse went on, "one er de ole fambly done come back 'long wid his daughter. Marse Briscoe Bascom en Miss Mildred dey done come back, en dey ain't got nobody fer ter he'p um out no way; en my ole 'oman she say dat ef I got any fambly feelin' I better go dar whar Marse Briscoe is."

For some time Major Jimmy Bass sat silent. He was shocked and stunned. Finally Jesse picked up his hat and cane and started to go. As he brushed his hat with his coat-sleeve his old master saw that he was rigged out in his Sunday clothes. As he moved away the major called him:—

"Oh, Jess!"

"Suh?"

"I allers knowed you was a durned fool, Jess, but I never did know before that you was the durndest fool in the universal world."

Jesse made no reply, and the major went into the house. When he told his wife

THE OLD BASCOM PLACE. 231

about Jesse's departure, that active-minded and sharp-tongued lady was very angry.

"Indeed, and I'm glad of it," she exclaimed as she poured out the major's coffee; "I'm truly glad of it. For twenty-five years that nigger has been laying around here doing nothing, and we a-paying him. But for pity's sake I'd 'a' drove him off the lot long ago. You may n't believe it, but that nigger is ready and willing to eat his own weight in vittles every week the Lord sends. I ain't sorry he's gone, but I'm sorry I did n't have a chance to give him a piece of my mind. Now, don't you go to blabbing it around, like you do everything else, that Jesse has gone and left us to go with old Briscoe Bascom."

Major Bass said he would n't, and he did n't, and that is the reason he expressed surprise when Joe-Bob Grissom informed him that Jesse was waiting on the old Judge and his daughter. Major Jimmy was talkative and fond of gossip, but he had too much respect for his wife's judgment and discretion to refuse to toe the mark, even when it was an imaginary one.

The Bascom family had no claim whatever on Jesse, but he had often heard his mother and other negroes boasting over that they had once belonged to the Bascoms, and fondness for the family was the result of both tradition and instinct. He had that undefined and undefinable respect for people of quality that is one of the virtues, or possibly one of the failings, of human nature. The nearest approach to people of quality, so far as his experience went, was to be found in the Bascom family, and he had never forgotten that he had belonged to an important branch of it. He held it as a sort of distinction. Feeling thus, it is no wonder that he was ready to leave a comfortable home at Major Jimmy Bass's for the privilege of attaching himself and his fortunes to those of the Judge and his daughter. Jesse made up his mind to take this step as soon as the Bascoms returned to Hillsborough, and he made no delay in carrying out his intentions.

Early one morning, not long after Judge Bascom and his daughter had settled themselves in the modest little house which they had selected because the rent was low, Mildred heard some one cutting wood in the yard. Opening her window blinds a little, she saw that the axe was wielded by a stal-

secret of its scantiness cropped out while the Judge and his daughter were eating.

"These biscuits are very well cooked. But there are too many of them. My daughter, we must pinch and save; it will only be for a little while. We must have the old Place back; we must rake and scrape, and save money and buy it back. And this coffee is very good, too," he went on; "it has quite the old flavor. I thought the girl was too young, but she's a good cook — a very good cook indeed."

Jesse, who had taken his stand behind the Judge's chair, arrayed in a snow-white apron, moved his body uneasily from one foot to the other. Mildred, glad to change the conversation, told her father about Jesse.

"Ah, yes," said Judge Bascom, in his kindly, patronizing way; "I saw him in the yard. And he used to belong to the Bascoms? Well, well, it must have been a long time ago. This is Jesse behind me? Stand out there, Jesse, and let me look at you. Ah, yes, a likely negro; a very likely negro indeed. And what Bascom did you belong to, Jesse? Merriwether Bascom! Why, to be sure; why, certainly!"

the Judge continued with as much animation as his feebleness would admit of. "Why, of course, Merriwether Bascom. Well, well, I remember him distinctly. A rough-and-tumble sort of man he was, fighting, gambling, horse-racing, always on the wing. A good man at bottom, but wild. And so you belonged to Merriwether Bascom? Well, boy, once a Bascom always a Bascom. We'll have the old Place back, Jesse, we'll have it back: but we must pinch ourselves; we must save."

Thus the old Judge rambled on in his talk. But no matter what the subject, no matter how far his memory and his experiences carried him away from the present, he was sure to return to the old Place at last. He must have it back. Every thought, every idea, was subordinate to this. He brooded over it and talked of it waking, and he dreamed of it sleeping. It was the one thought that dominated every other. Money must be saved, the old Place must be bought, and to that end everything must tend. The more his daughter economized the more he urged her to economize. His earnestness and enthusiasm impressed and influenced the young girl in a larger measure than she would have been willing to acknowledge, and unconsciously she found herself looking forward to the day when her father and herself would be able to call the Bascom Place their own. In the Judge the thought was the delusion of old age, in the maiden it was the dream of youth; and pardonable, perhaps, in both.

Their hopes and desires running thus in one channel, they loved to wander of an evening in the neighborhood of the old Place — it was just in the outskirts of the town — and long for the time when they should take possession of their home. On these occasions Mildred, by way of interesting her father, would suggest changes to be made.

"The barn is painted red," she would say. "I think olive green would be prettier."

"No," the Judge would reply; "we will have the barn removed. It was not there in my time. It is an innovation. We will have it removed a mile away from the house. We will make many changes. There are hundreds of acres in the meadow yonder that ought to be in cotton. In my time we tried to kill grass, but this man is doing his best to propagate it. Look at that field of Bermuda there. Two years of hard work will be required to get the grass out."

Once while the Judge and his daughter were passing by the old Place they met Prince, the mastiff, in the road. The great dog looked at the young lady with kindly eyes, and expressed his approval by wagging his tail. Then he approached and allowed her to fondle his lionlike head, and walked by her side, responding to her talk in a dumb but eloquent way. Prince evidently thought that the young lady and her father were going in the avenue gate and to the house, for when they got nearly opposite, the dog trotted on ahead, looking back occasionally, as if by that means to extend them an invitation and to assure them that they were welcome. At the gate he stopped and turned around, and seeing that the fair lady and the old gentleman were going by, he dropped his bulky body on the ground in a disconsolate way and watched them as they passed down the street.

The next afternoon Prince made it a point to watch for the young lady; and when she and her father appeared in sight he ran to meet them and cut up such unusual capers, barking and running around, that his master went down the avenue to see what the trouble was. Mr. Underwood took off his hat as Judge Bascom and his daughter drew near.

"This is Judge Bascom, I presume," he said. "My name is Underwood. I am glad to meet you."

"This is my daughter, Mr. Underwood," said the Judge, bowing with great dignity.

"My dog has paid you a great compliment, Miss Bascom," said Francis Underwood. "He makes few friends, and I have never before seen him sacrifice his dignity to his enthusiasm."

"I feel highly flattered by his attentions," said Mildred, laughing. "I have read somewhere, or heard it said, that the instincts of a little child and a dog are unerring."

"I imagine," said the Judge, in his dignified way, "that instinct has little to do with the matter. I prefer to believe" — He paused a moment, looked at Underwood, and laid his hand on the young man's stalwart shoulder. "Did you know, sir," he went on, "that this place, all these lands, once belonged to me?" His dignity had vanished, his whole attitude changed. The pathos in his voice, which was suggested rather than expressed, swept away whatever astonishment Francis Underwood might have felt. The young man looked at the Judge's daughter and their eyes met. In that one glance, transitory though it was, he found his cue; in her lustrous eyes, proud yet appealing, he read a history of trouble and sacrifice.

"Yes," Underwood replied, in a matter-of-fact way. "I knew the place once belonged to you, and I have been somewhat proud of the fact. We still call it the Bascom Place, you know."

"I should think so!" exclaimed the Judge, bridling up a little; "I should think so! Pray what else could it be called?"

"Well, it might have been called Grasslands, you know, or The Poplars, but somehow the old name seemed to suit it best. I like to think of it as the Bascom Place."

"You are right, sir," said the Judge with emphasis; "you are right, sir. It is the Bascom Place. All the powers of earth cannot strip us of our name."

Again Underwood looked at the young girl, and again he read in her shining but apprehensive eyes the answer he should make.

"I have been compelled to add some conveniences — I will not call them improvements — and I have made some repairs, but I have tried to preserve the main and familiar features of the Place."

"But the barn there; that is not where it should be. It should be a mile away — on the creek."

"That would improve appearances, no doubt; but if you were to get out at four or five o'clock in the morning and see to the milking of twelve or fifteen cows, I dare say you would wish the barn even nearer than it is."

"Yes, yes, I suppose so," responded the Judge; "yes, no doubt. But it was not there in my time — not in my time."

"I have some very fine cows," Underwood went on. "Won't you go in and look at them? I think they would interest Miss Bascom, and my sister would be glad to meet her. Won't you go in, sir, and look at the old house?"

The Judge turned his pale and wrinkled face towards his old home.

"No," he said, "not now. I thank you very much. I — somehow — no, sir, I cannot go now."

His hand shook as he raised it to his face, and his lips trembled as he spoke.

"Let us go home, daughter," he said after a while. "We have walked far enough." He bowed to young Underwood, and Mildred bade him good-bye with a troubled smile.

Prince went with them a little way down the street. He walked by the side of the lady, and her pretty hand rested lightly on the dog's massive head. It was a beautiful picture, Underwood thought, as he stood watching them pass out of sight.

"You are a lucky dog," he said to Prince when the latter came back, "but you don't appreciate your privileges. If you did you would have gone home with that lovely woman." Prince wagged his tail, but it is doubtful if he fully understood the remark.

V.

One Sunday morning, as Major Jimmy Bass was shaving himself, he heard a knock at the back door. The major had his coat and waistcoat off and his suspenders were hanging around his hips. He was applying the lather for the last time, and the knocking was so sudden and unexpected that he rubbed the shaving-brush in one of his eyes. He began to make some remarks which, however appropriate they may have been to the occasion, could not be reported here with propriety. But in the midst of his indignant monologue he remembered that the knocking might have proceeded from some of Mrs. Bass's lady friends, who frequently made a descent on the premises in that direction for the purpose of borrowing a cupful of sugar or coffee in a social way. These considerations acted as powerful brakes on the conversation that Major Bass was carrying on with some imaginary foe. Holding a towel to his smarting eye, he peeped from his room door and looked down the hall. The back door was open, but he could see no one.

"Who was that knocking?" he cried. "I'll go one eye on you anyways."

"'T ain't nobody but me, Marse Maje," came the response from the door.

"Is that you, Jess?" exclaimed the major. "Well, pleg-take your hide to the pleg-taked nation! A little more an' you'd 'a' made me cut my th'oat from year to year; an' as it is, I've jest about got enough soap in my eye fer to do a day's washin'."

"Is you shavin' yourse'f, Marse Maje?" asked Jesse, diplomatically.

"That I am," replied the major with emphasis. "I allers was independent of white folks, an' sence you pulled up your stakes an' took up wi' the quality I'm about independent of the niggers. An' it's mighty quare to me," the major went on, "that you'd leave your high an' mighty people long enough fer to come a-bangin' an' makin' me put out my eyes. Why, ef I'd 'a' had my razor out, I'll be boun' you'd made me cut my th'oat, an' much good may it 'a' done you."

"Name er goodness, Marse Maje," protested Jesse, "what make you go on dat a-way? Ef I'd 'a' knowed you wuz busy in dar I'd 'a' set out in de sun en waited twel you got thoo."

"Yes," said the major in a sarcastic but somewhat mollified tone, "you'd 'a' sot out there an' got to noddin', an' then bimeby your Miss Sarah would 'a' come along an' ketched you there, an' I'll be boun' she'd 'a' lammed you wi' a chunk of wood; bekaze she don't 'low no loafin' in the back yard sence you been gone. I don't know what you come fer," the major continued, still wiping the lather out of his eye, "an' nuther do I keer; but sence you are here you kin come in an' finish shavin' me, fer to pay fer the damage you 've done."

Jesse was apparently overjoyed to find that he could be of some service. He bustled around in the liveliest manner, and was soon mowing the major's fat face with the light but firm touch for which he was noted. As he shaved he talked.

"Marse Maje," he said, "does you know what I come fer dis mornin'?"

"I 've been tryin' to think," replied the major; "but I could n't tell you ef I was a-gwine to be hung fer it. You are up to some devilment, I know mighty well, but I wish 't I may die ef I 've got any idee what it is."

"Now, Marse Maje, what make you talk dat'a'way?"

"Oh, I know you, Jess, an' I 've been a-knowin' you a mighty long time. Your Miss Sarah may n't know you, Jess, but I know you from the groun' all the way up."

Jesse laughed. He was well aware that the major's wife was the knowing one of that family. He had waited until that excellent lady had issued from the house on her way to church, and it was not until she was out of sight that he thought it safe to call on the major. Even now, after he had found the major alone, the negro was somewhat doubtful as to the propriety of explaining the nature of his business; but the old man was inquisitive.

"Oh, yes, Jess!" the major went on, after pausing long enough to have the corner of his mouth shaved — "oh, yes! I know you, an' I know you've got somethin' on your min' right now. Spit it out."

"Well, I'll tell you de trufe, Marse Maje," said Jesse, after hesitating for some time; "I tell you de Lord's trufe, I come yer atter somepin' ter eat."

Major Bass caught the negro by the arm, pushed the razor carefully out of the way, and sat bolt upright in the chair.

"Do you mean to stan' up there, you triflin' rascal," the major exclaimed, "an' tell me, right before my face an' eyes, that you've come a-sneaking back here atter vittles? Why n't you stay where the vittles was?" Major Bass was really indignant.

"Wait, Marse Maje; des gimme time," said Jesse, nervously strapping the razor on the palm of his hand. "Des gimme time,"

Marse Maje. You fly up so, suh, dat you git me all mixed up wid myse'f. I come atter vittles, dat's de Lord's trufe; but I ain't come atter 'em fer myse'f. Nigger like me don't stay hongry long roun' whar folks know um like dey does me."

"Well, who in the name of reason sent you, then?" asked the major.

"Nobody ain't sont me, suh," said Jesse.

"Well, who do you want em' fer?" insisted the major.

"Marse Judge Bascom en Miss Mildred," replied Jesse solemnly.

Major Jimmy Bass fell back in his chair in a state of collapse, overcome by his astonment.

"*Well!*" he exclaimed, as soon as he could catch his breath. "Ef this don't beat the Jews an' the Gentiles, the Scribes an' the Pharisees, then I ain't a-settin' here. Did they tell you to come to this house fer vittles?"

"No, suh; *dat* dey ain't — *dat* dey ain't! Ef Miss Mildred wuz ter know I went anywhar on dis kin' er errun' she'd mighty nigh have a fit."

"Well, *well*, WELL!" snorted the major.

"I des come my own se'f," Jesse went

on. He would have begun shaving again, but the major waved him away. "Look like I 'bleege' ter come. You'd 'a' come yo'se'f, Marse Maje, druther dan see dem folks pe'sh deyse'f ter deff. Dey got money, but Marse Judge Bascom got de idee dat dey hafter save it all fer ter buy back de ole Place. Dey pinch deyse'f day in en day out, en yistiddy when Miss Mildred say she gwine buy somepin' fer Sunday, Marse Judge Bascom he say no; he 'low dat dey mus' save en pinch en buy back de ole home. I done year him say dat twel it make me plum sick. An' dar dey is naturally starvin' deyse'f.

"Miss Mildred," continued Jesse, "got idee dat her pa know what he talkin' 'bout; but twix' you en me, Marse Maje, dat ole man done about lose his min'. He ain't so mighty much older dan what you is, but he mighty feeble in his limbs, en he mighty flighty in his head. He talk funny, now, en he don't talk 'bout nothin' skacely but buyin' back the ole Place."

"Jess," said Major Bass in the smooth, insinuating tone that the negro knew so well, and that he had learned to fear, "ain't I allers treated you right? Ain't I allers done the clean thing by you?"

"Yes, Marse Maje, you is," said the negro with emphasis.

"Well, then, Jess, what in the name of Moses do you want to come roun' me wi' such a tale as this? Don't you know I know you clean through? Why n't you come right out an' say you want the vittles fer yourself? What is the use whippin' the devil 'roun' the stump?"

"Marse Maje," said Jesse, solemnly, "I'm a-tellin' you de Lord's trufe." By this time he had begun to shave the major again.

"Well," said Major Bass, after a pause, during which he seemed to be thinking, "suppos'n' I was to let myself be took in by your tale, an' suppos'n' I was to give you some vittles, what have you got to put 'em in?"

"I got a basket out dar, Marse Maje," said Jesse, cheerfully. "I brung it a purpose."

"Why, tooby shore, tooby shore!" exclaimed the major, sarcastically. "Ef you was as forehanded as you is fore-thoughted you would n't be a-runnin' roun' beggin' vittles from han' to mouth. But sence you are here you'd better make haste; bekaze ef your

Miss Sarah comes back from church and ketches you here, she'll kick up a purty rippit."

The major was correct. As he and Jesse went into the pantry Mrs. Bass entered the front door. Flinging her bonnet and mantilla on a bed, she went to the back porch for a drink of water. The major heard her coming through the hallway, and, by a swift gesture of his hand, cautioned Jesse to be quiet.

"I'll vow if the place ain't left to take care of itself," Mrs. Bass was saying. "Doors all open, chickens in the dining-room, cat licking the churn-dasher, and I'll bet my existence that not a drop of fresh water has been put in the house-bucket since I left this morning. Everything gone to rack and ruin. I can't say my prayers in peace at home, and if I go to church one Sunday in a month there ain't no satisfaction in the sermon, because I know everything's at loose ends on this whole blessed place. And if you'd go up the street right now, you'd find Mr. Bass a-setting up there at the tavern with the other loafers, a-giggling and a-snickering and a-dribbling at the mouth like one possessed."

The major, in the pantry, winced visibly at this picture drawn true to life, and as he attempted to change his position he knocked a tin vessel from one of the shelves. He caught at it, and it fell to the floor with a loud crash.

"The Lord have mercy!" exclaimed Mrs. Bass. "Is Satan and all his imps in the pantry, a-tearing down and a-smashing up things?" Not being a timid woman, she hastened to investigate. The sight she saw in the pantry struck her speechless. In one corner stood the major, holding up one foot, as if he was afraid of breaking something, and vainly trying to smile. In another corner stood Jesse, so badly frightened that very little could be seen of his face except the whites of his eyes. The tableau was a comical one. Mrs. Bass did not long remain speechless.

"Mr. Bass!" she exclaimed, "what under the shining sun are you doing colloguing with niggers in my pantry? If you want to collogue with niggers, why, in the name of common sense, don't you take 'em out to the barn? What are you doing in there, anyhow? For mercy's sake! have you gone stark-natural crazy? And if you ain't, what brand-new caper are you trying to cut up?"

"Don't talk so loud, Sarah," said the major, wiping the cold perspiration from his face. "All the neighbors 'll hear you."

"And why shouldn't they hear me?" exclaimed Mrs. Bass. "What could be worse than for me to come home from church in broad daylight and find you penned up in my pantry, arm-in-arm with a nigger? What business have you got with niggers that you have to take 'em into my pantry to collogue with 'em? I'd a heap rather you 'd 'a' taken 'em in the parlor — a heap rather."

Then Mrs. Bass's eyes fell on the basket Jesse had in his hand, and this added to her indignation.

"I believe in my soul," she went on, "that you are stealing the meat and bread out of your own mouth to feed that nigger. If you ain't, what is the basket for?"

"Tut, tut, Sarah, don't you go on so; you 'll make yourself the laughin'-stock of the town," said the major in a conciliatory tone.

"And what 'll you be?" continued Mrs. Bass, relentlessly; "what 'll you be — a honeyin' up with buck niggers in my pantry in the broad open daytime? Maybe you'll have the manners to introduce me to your pardner. Who is he, anyhow?" Then Mrs. Bass turned her attention to the negro.

"Come out of my pantry, you nasty, trifling rascal! Who are you?"

"'T ain't nobody but me, Miss Sa'ah," said Jesse as he issued forth.

"You!" she exclaimed. "You are the nigger that was too biggity to stay with 'em that raised you up and took care of you, and now you come back and try to steal their bread and meat! Well! I know the end of the world ain't so mighty far off."

Mrs. Bass sank into a chair, exhausted by her indignation. Then the major took the floor, so to say, and showed that if he could be frightened by his wife, he could also, at the proper time, show that he had a will of his own. He explained the situation at some length, and with an emphasis that carried conviction with it. He made no mention of Jesse in his highly colored narrative, but left his wife to infer that while she was at church praying for peace of mind and not having her prayers answered to any great extent, he was at home engaged in works of practical charity. Nothing could have been finer than the major's air of injured innocence, unless it was Jesse's attitude of helpless and abandoned humiliation. The result of it was that Mrs. Bass filled the basket with the best she had in the house, and Jesse went home happy.

VI.

As for the Bascoms, they seemed to be getting along comfortably in spite of the harrowing story that Jesse had told to Major Jimmy Bass and to others. As a matter of fact, the shrewd negro had purposely exaggerated the condition of affairs in the Bascom household. He had an idea that the fare they lived on was too common and cheap for the representatives of such a grand family, forgetting, or not knowing, the privations they had passed through. The Judge insisted on the most rigid economy, and Mildred was at one with him in this. She was familiar with the necessity for it, but she could see that her father was anxious to push it to unmeasurable lengths. It never occurred to her, however, that her father's morbid anxiety to repossess the

Bascom Place was rapidly taking the shape of mania. This desire on the part of Judge Bascom was a part of his daughter's life. She had heard it expressed in various ways ever since she could remember, and it was a part, not merely of her experience, but of her growth and development. She had heard the matter discussed so many times that it seemed to her nothing but natural that her father should one day realize the dream of his later years and reoccupy the old Place as proprietor.

Judge Bascom had no other thought than this. As he grew older and feebler, the desire became more ardent and overpowering. While his daughter was teaching her school, with which she had made quite a success, the Judge would be planning improvements to be added to his old home when he should own it again. Not a day passed — unless, indeed, the weather was stormy — that he did not walk in the neighborhood of the old Place. Sometimes he would go with his daughter, sometimes he would go alone, but it was observed by those who came to be interested in his comings and goings that he invariably refused to accept the invitation of Mr. Underwood to enter the house or to inspect the improvements that had been made. He persisted in remaining on the outside of the domain, content to wait for the day when he could enter as proprietor. He was willing to accept the position of spectator, but he was not willing to be a guest.

The culmination came one fine day in the fall, and it was so sudden and so peculiar that it took Hillsborough completely by surprise, and gave the people food for gossip for a long time afterwards. The season was hesitating as to whether summer should return or winter should be introduced. There was a hint of winter in the crisp morning breezes, but the world seemed to float summerwards in the glimmering haze that wrapped the hills in the afternoons. On one of these fine mornings Judge Bascom rose and dressed himself. His daughter heard him humming a tune as he walked about the room, and she observed also, with inward satisfaction, that his movements were brisker than usual. Listening a little attentively, she heard him talking to himself, and presently she heard him laugh. This was such an unusual occurrence that she was moved to knock at his door. He responded with a cheery "Come in!" Mildred found him shaved and dressed, and she saw that there was a great change in his appearance. His cheeks, usually so wan and white, were flushed a little and his eyes were bright. He smiled as Mildred entered, and exclaimed in a tone that she had not heard for years: —

"Good-morning, my daughter! And how do you find yourself this morning?"

It was the old manner she used to admire so when she was a slip of a girl — a manner that was a charming combination of dignity and affection.

"Why, father!" she exclaimed, "you must be feeling better. You have positively grown younger in a night."

The Judge laughed until his eyes sparkled. "Yes, my dear, I am feeling very well indeed. I never felt better. I am happy, quite happy. Everything has been made clear to me. I am going to-day to transact some business that has been troubling me a long time. I shall arrange it all to-day — yes, to-day."

The change that had come over her father was such a relief to Mildred that she asked him no questions. Now, as always, she trusted to his judgment and his experience. Jesse, however, was more critical. He watched the Judge furtively and shook his head.

"Mistiss," he said to Mildred when he found an opportunity, "did you shave master?"

"Why, what a ridiculous question!" she exclaimed. "How could I shave him? It makes me shiver merely to touch the razors."

"Well, Mistiss," Jesse insisted, "ef I ain't shave him, en you ain't shave him, den who de name er goodness is done gone en done it?"

"He shaved himself, of course," Mildred said. "He is very much better this morning. I noticed it the moment I saw him. I should think you could see it yourself."

"I seed somepin' nuther wuz de matter," said Jesse. "Somepin' 'bleege' ter be de matter when I put him ter bed las' night des like he wuz a baby, ma'm, en now yer he is gwine roun' des ez spry ez de nex' one. Yessum, somepin' 'bleege' ter be de matter. Yistiddy his han's wuz shakin' same like he got de polzy, ma'm, en now yer he is shavin' hisse'f; dat what rack my min'."

"Well, I hope you are glad he is so well, Jesse," said Mildred in an injured tone.

"Oh, yessum," said Jesse, scratching his head. "Lor', yessum. Dey ain't nobody no gladder dan what I is; but it come on me so sudden, ma'm, dat it sorter skeer me."

"Well, it does n't frighten me," said Mildred. "It makes me very happy."

"Yessum," replied Jesse deferentially. He made no further comment; but after Mildred had gone to attend to her school duties he made it his business to keep an eye on the Judge, and the closer the negro watched, the more forcibly was he struck by the great change that a night had made in the old man.

"I hear talk 'bout folks bein' conjured inter sickness," Jesse said to himself, "but I ain't never hear talk 'bout dey bein' conjured so dey git well."

Certainly a great change had come over Judge Bascom. He stood firmly on his feet once more. He held his head erect, as in the old days, and when he talked to Jesse his tone was patronizing and commanding, instead of querulous and complaining. He seemed to be very fastidious about his appearance. After Mildred had gone to her school, Jesse was called in to brush the Judge's hat and coat and to polish his shoes. The Judge watched this process with great interest, and talked to the negro in his blandest manner. This was not so surprising to Jesse as the fact that the Judge persisted in calling him Wesley; Wesley was the Judge's old body-servant who had been dead for twenty years. It was Wesley this and Wesley that so long as Jesse was in the room, and once the Judge asked how long before the carriage would be ready. The negro parried this question, but he remembered it. He was sorely puzzled an hour afterwards, however, when Judge Bascom called him and said: —

"Wesley, tell Jordan he need not bring the carriage around for me. I will walk. Jordan can bring your mistress when she is ready."

"Well," exclaimed Jesse, when the Judge disappeared in the house, "dis bangs me! What de name er goodness put de ole man Jerd'n in his min', which he died endurance er de war? It's all away beyant me. Miss Mildred oughter be yer wid her pa right now, yit, ef I go atter her, dey ain't no tellin' what he gwine do."

Jess cut an armful of wood, and then made a pretense of washing dishes, going from the kitchen to the dining-room several times. More than once he stopped to listen, but he could hear nothing. After a while he made bold to peep into the sitting-room. There was nobody there. He went into the Judge's bedroom; it was empty. Then he called — "Marster! oh, Marster!" but there was no reply. Jess was in a quandary. He was not alarmed, but he was uneasy.

"Ef I run en tell Miss Mildred dat Marster done gone som'ers," he said to himself, "she'll des laugh en say I ain't got no sense; en I don't speck I is, but it make my flesh crawl fer ter hear folks callin' on dead niggers ter do dis en do dat."

Meanwhile the Judge had sallied forth from the house, and was proceeding in the direction of the Bascom Place. His step was firm and elastic, his bearing dignified. The acquaintances whom he met on his way stopped and looked after him when they had returned his Chesterfieldian salutation. He walked rapidly, and there was an air of decision in his movements that had long been lacking. At the great gate opening into the avenue of the Bascom Place the Judge was met by Prince the mastiff, who gave him a hospitable welcome, and gravely preceded him to the house. Miss Sophie, Mr. Underwood's maiden sister, who was sitting in the piazza, engaged on some kind of feminine embroidery, saw the Judge coming, too late to beat a retreat, so she merely whipped behind one of the large pillars, gave her dress a little shake at the sides and behind, ran her hands over her hair, and appeared before the caller cool, calm, and collected.

"Good-morning, madam," said the Judge in his grand way, taking off his hat.

"Good-morning, sir," said Miss Sophie. "Have this chair?"

"No, no," said the Judge, smiling blandly, and waving his hand. "I prefer my own chair — the large rocker with the cushion, you know. It is more comfortable."

Somewhat puzzled, Miss Sophie fetched a rocker. It had no cushion, but the Judge seemed not to miss it.

"Why, where are the servants?" he asked, his brows contracting a little. "I could have brought the chair."

"Mercy!" exclaimed Miss Sophie, "if I were to sit down and expect the negroes to wait on me, I'd have a good many disappointments during the day."

"Yes," said the Judge, "that is very true; very true. Where is Wesley?"

"I'm sure I don't know," Miss Sophie replied. "Is he a white man or a negro?"

"Wesley?" exclaimed the Judge. "Why, he's a nigger; he's my body-servant."

"Isn't this Judge Bascom?" Miss Sophie inquired, regarding him curiously.

"Yes, certainly, madam," responded the Judge.

"Well, I've seen a negro named Jesse following you and your daughter about," said Miss Sophie. "Perhaps you are speaking of Jesse."

"No, no," said the Judge. "I mean Wesley — or maybe you are only a visitor here. Your face is familiar, but I have forgotten your name."

"I am Francis Underwood's sister," said Miss Sophie, with some degree of pride.

"Ah, yes!" the Judge sighed — "Francis Underwood. He is the gentleman who has had charge of the place these several years. A very clever man, I have no doubt. He has done very well, very well indeed; better than most men would have done. Do you know where he will go next year?"

"Now, I couldn't tell you, really," Miss

Sophie replied, looking at the Judge through her gold-rimmed eye-glasses. "He did intend to go North this fall, but he's always too busy to carry out his intentions."

"Yes," said Judge Bascom; "I have no doubt he is a very busy man. He has managed everything very cleverly here, and I wish him well wherever he goes."

Miss Sophie was very glad when she heard her brother's step in the hall; not that she was nervous or easily frightened, but there was something in Judge Bascom's actions, something in the tone of his voice, some suggestion in his words, that gave her uneasiness, and she breathed a sigh of relief when her stalwart brother made his appearance.

Francis Underwood greeted his guest cordially — more cordially, Miss Sophie thought, than circumstances warranted; but the beautiful face of Mildred Bascom was not stamped on Miss Sophie's mind as it was on her brother's.

"I am sorry to put you to any inconvenience," said the Judge, after they had talked for some time on commonplace topics — "very sorry. I have put the matter off until at last I felt it to be a solemn duty I

THE OLD BASCOM PLACE. 265

owed my family to come here. Believe me, sir," he continued, turning to the young man with some emotion — "believe me, sir, it grieves me to trouble you in the matter, but I could no longer postpone coming here. I think I understand and appreciate your attachment" —

"Why, my dear sir," cried Francis Underwood in his heartiest manner, "it is no trouble at all. No one could be more welcome here. I have often wondered why you have never called before. Don't talk about trouble and inconvenience."

"I think I understand and appreciate your attachment for the Place," the Judge went on as though he had not been interrupted, "and it embarrasses me, I assure you, to be compelled to trouble you now."

"Well," said Francis Underwood, with a hospitable laugh, "if it is no trouble to you, it certainly is none to me. As my neighbors around here say, when I call on them, 'just make yourself at home.'"

Judge Bascom rose from his chair trembling. He seemed suddenly to be laboring under the most intense excitement.

"My home?" he almost shrieked — "make myself at home! In God's name, man, what can you mean? It *is* my home! It has always been my home! Everything here is mine — every foot of land, every tree, every brick and stone and piece of timber in this house. It is *all* mine, and I will have it! I have come here to assert my rights!"

He panted with passion and excitement as he looked from Francis Underwood to Miss Sophie. He paused, as if daring them to dispute his claims. Miss Sophie, who had a temper of her own, would have given the Judge a piece of her mind, but she saw her brother regarding the old man with a puzzled, pitying expression. Then the truth flashed on her, and for an instant she felt like crying. Francis Underwood approached the Judge and led him gently back to his chair.

"Now that you are at home, Judge Bascom," he said, "you need not worry yourself."

"I tell you it is *mine!*" the Judge went on, beating the arm of his chair with his clenched fist; "it is mine. It has always been mine, and it will always be mine."

Francis Underwood stood before the old man, active, alert, smiling. His sister said afterwards that she was surprised at the prompt gentleness with which her brother disposed of what promised to be a very disagreeable scene.

"Judge Bascom," said the young man, swinging himself around on his boot-heels, "as your guest here, allow me to suggest that you ought to show me over the place. I have been told you have some very fine cows here."

Immediately Judge Bascom was himself again. His old air of dignity returned, and he became in a moment the affable host.

"As my guests here," he said, smiling with pleasure, "you and the lady are very welcome. We keep open house at the Bascom Place, and we are glad to have our friends with us. What we have is yours. I suppose," he went on, still smiling, "some of our neighbors have been joking about our cows. We have a good many of them, but they don't amount to much. They have been driven to the pasture by this time, and that is on the creek a mile and a half from here. I wonder where Wesley is! I think he is growing more worthless every year. He ought to be here with my daughter. The carriage was sent for her some time ago."

"I will see if he is in the yard," said Underwood, and his sister followed him through the hall.

"Mercy!" Miss Sophie exclaimed when they were out of hearing; "does the old Judge purpose to swarm and settle down on us?" She had an economical turn of mind. "What in the world is the matter with him?"

"I pity him from the bottom of my heart," said Francis Underwood, "but I am sorrier for his daughter. Everything seems to be blotted out of his mind except the notion that he is the owner of this Place. We must humor him, sister, and we must be tender with the daughter. You know how to do that much better than I do."

Miss Sophie frowned a little. The situation was a new and trying one, but she had been confronted with emergencies before, and her experience and her strong common sense stood her in good stead now. With a woman's promptness she decided on a line of action at once sympathetic and effectual. The buggy was ordered out and young Underwood went for a physician.

Then, when he had returned, Miss Sophie said he must go for the daughter, and she cautioned him, with some severity of manner, as to what he should say and how he should deport himself. But at this Francis Underwood rebelled. Ordinarily he was a very agreeable and accommodating young fellow, but when his sister informed him that he must fetch Mildred Bascom to her father, he pulled off his hat and scratched his blond head in perplexity.

"What could I say, sister?" he protested. "How could I explain the situation? No; it is a woman's work, and you must go. It would be a pretty come-off for me to go after this poor girl and in a fit of awkwardness frighten her to death. It is bad enough as it is. There is no hurry. You shall have the carriage. It would never do for me to go; no one but a woman knows how to be sympathetic in a matter of this kind."

"I never knew before that you were so bashful," said Miss Sophie, regarding him keenly. "It is a recent development."

"It is not bashfulness, sister," said Underwood, coloring a little. "It is consideration. How could I explain matters to this poor girl? How could I prevail on her to come here without giving her an inkling of the situation, and thus frighten her, perhaps unnecessarily?"

"Perhaps you are right," said Miss Sophie, who, as an experienced spinster, was not always ready to make concessions of this kind. "At any rate I'll go for Miss Bascom, and I think I can manage it without alarming her; but the matter troubles me. I hope the poor old Judge will not be a dangerous guest."

"There is not the slightest fear of that," said Francis Underwood. "He is too feeble for that. When I placed my hand on his shoulder just now he was all of a tremble. He is no stronger than a little child, and no more dangerous. Besides, the doctor is with him."

"Well," said Miss Sophie with a sigh, "I'll go. Women are compelled to do most of the odd jobs that men are afraid to take up; but I shiver to think of it. I shall surely break down when I see that poor child."

"No," said her brother, "you will not. I know you too well for that. We must humor this old man, and that will be for me to do; his daughter must be left to you."

VII.

ALL this was no less the result of Francis Underwood's desire than of the doctor's commands. The old practitioner was noted for his skill throughout the region, and after he had talked with Judge Bascom he gave it as his opinion that the only physic necessary in the case was perfect rest and quiet, and that these could be secured only by allowing the old man to remain undisturbed in the belief that he was once more the owner of the Bascom Place.

"He'll not trouble you for long," said Dr. Bynum, wiping his spectacles, "and I've no doubt that whatever expense may be incurred will be settled by his old friends. Oh, Bascom still has friends here," exclaimed the doctor, misunderstanding Underwood's gesture of protest. "He went wrong, badly wrong; but he is a Southerner, sir, to the very core, and in the South we are in the habit of looking after our own. We may differ, sir, but when the pinch comes you'll find us together."

The doctor's lofty air was wholly lost on his companion.

"My dear sir," said Underwood, laying his hand somewhat heavily on the doctor's shoulder, "what do you take me for? Do you suppose that I intend to set up a hospital here?"

"Oh, by no means, by no means," said Dr. Bynum, soothingly. "Not at all; in fact, quite the contrary. As I say, you shall be reimbursed for all" —

"Dr. Bynum," said Underwood, with some degree of emphasis, "permit me to remind you that Judge Bascom is my guest. There is no question of money except so far as your bill is concerned, and that" —

"Now, now, my *dear* boy," exclaimed the old doctor, holding up both hands in a gesture of expostulation, "don't, *don't* fly up! What is the use? I was only explaining matters; I was only trying to let you know how we Southerners feel. You must have noticed that the poor old Judge has n't been treated very well since his return here. His best friends have avoided him. I was only trying to tell you that they hold him in high esteem, and that they are willing to do all they can for him."

"As a Southerner?" inquired Underwood, "or as a man?"

"Tut, tut!" exclaimed Dr. Bynum. "Don't come running at me with your head down and your horns up. We've no time to fall into a dispute. You look after the Judge as a Northerner, and I'll look after him as a Southerner. His daughter must come here. He is very feeble. He has but one irrational idea, and that is that he owns the old Place. In every other particular his mind is sound, and he will give you no trouble. His idea must be humored, and even then the collapse will come too soon for that poor girl, his daughter — as lovely a creature, sir, as you ever saw."

This statement was neither information nor news so far as Underwood was concerned. "If I see her," the old doctor went on, with a somewhat patronizing air, "I'll try to explain matters; but it is a very delicate undertaking, sir — very delicate."

"No," said Underwood; "there will be no need for explanations. My sister will go for Miss Bascom, and whatever explanations may be necessary she will make at the proper time."

"An admirable arrangement," said Dr. Bynum with a grunt of satisfaction — "an admirable arrangement indeed. Well, my boy, you must do the best you can, and I know that will be all that is necessary. I am sorry for Bascom, very sorry, and I 'm sorrier for his daughter. I 'll call again to-night."

As Dr. Bynum drove down the avenue, Underwood was much gratified to see Jesse coming through the gate. The negro appeared to be much perplexed. He took off his hat as he approached Underwood, and made a display of politeness somewhat unusual, although he was always polite.

"Is you seed Marse Judge Bascom?" he inquired.

"Yes," said Underwood. "He is in the house yonder, resting himself. You seem frightened; what is the trouble?"

"Well, suh, I ain't had no such worriment sence de Sherman army come 'long. I dunner what got inter Marse Judge Bascom. He been gwine on des like yuther folks, settin' 'roun' en talkin' 'long wid hisse'f, en den all of er sudden he break out en shave en dress hisse'f, en go visitin' whar he ain't never been visitin' befo'. I done year 'im say p'intedly dat he ain't never gwine come yer les'n de Place b'long ter 'im. Do he look downhearted, suh?"

"No," said Underwood, "I can't say that he does. He seems to be very well satisfied. He has called several times for Wesley. I have heard you called Jesse, but perhaps the Judge knows you as Wesley. There are several negroes around here who answer to different names."

"No, suh," said Jesse, scratching his head. "I ain't never been call Wesley sence I been bornded inter de worl'. Dey was er nigger name Wesley what use ter go 'long wid Marse Judge Bascom en wait on 'im when I wuz er little boy, but Wesley done been dead too long ago ter talk about. I dunner what make folks's min' drop back dat 'a'way. Look like dey er sorter fumblin' 'roun' tryin' fer ter ketch holt er sump'n ne'r what done been pulled up out'n reach."

"Well," said Underwood, "the Judge is in the house. See if he wants anything; and if he asks about his daughter, tell him she will be here directly."

When Jesse went into the house he found the Judge lying on a lounge in the hall. His eyes were closed, and he seemed to be dozing; but Jesse's movements aroused him.

"Ah! is that you, Wesley? Where is your Miss Mildred?"

"She comin', suh; she comin' right now."

"Very well, very well. You must make yourself at home here," he said to Francis Underwood, who had followed Jesse. "I am somewhat dilapidated myself, but my daughter will entertain you. Wesley, I believe I will go to my room. Lend me your arm."

"Allow me to assist you," said Underwood; and so between the two the old man was carried to the room that had been his own when the house was his. It happened to be Underwood's room, but that made no difference. It belonged once more to the Judge in his disordered fancy, and thither he went.

After a while Miss Sophie came, bringing Mildred. Just how she had explained matters to the poor girl no one ever knew, but it must have been in some specially sympathetic way, for when Francis Underwood assisted the ladies from the carriage Miss Bascom appeared to be the less agitated of the two.

"The Judge is as comfortable as possible," Underwood said cheerily. "Jesse is with him, and I think he is asleep. His nervousness has passed away."

"Oh, do you think he is seriously ill?" exclaimed Mildred, clasping her hands together.

"Certainly not, just now," said Francis Underwood. "The doctor has been here, and he has gone away apparently satisfied. Sister, do you take charge of Miss Bascom, and show her how to be at home here."

And so Judge Bascom and his beautiful daughter were installed at the old Place. Mildred, under the circumstances, would rather have been elsewhere, but she was practically under orders. It was necessary to the well-being of her father, so the doctor said, that he should remain where he was; it was necessary that he should be humored in the belief that he was the owner of the old Place. It is only fair to say that Miss Sophie Underwood and her brother were more willing and anxious to enter into this scheme than Mildred appeared to be. She failed to comprehend the situation until after she had talked with her father, and then she was in despair. Judge Bascom was the representative of everything substantial and enduring in his daughter's experience, and when she realized that his mind had been seized by a vagary she received a tremendous shock. But the rough edges of the situation, so to speak, were smoothed and turned by Miss Sophie, who assumed motherly charge of the young girl. Miss Sophie's methods were so sympathetic and so womanly, and she gave to the situation such a matter-of-fact interpretation, that the grief and dismay of the young girl were not as overwhelming as they otherwise would have been.

VIII.

Naturally all the facts that have just been set down here were soon known to the inhabitants of Hillsborough. Naturally, too, something more than the facts was also known and talked about. There was the good old doctor ready to shake his head and look mysterious, and there were the negroes ready to give out an exaggerated version of the occurrences that followed Judge Bascom's visit to his old home.

"Well," said Major Jimmy Bass to his wife, with something like a snort, "ef the old Judge is gone there an' took holt of things, like they say, it's bekaze he's out 'n his mind. I wonder what in the round world could 'a' possessed him?"

"I 'spec' he's done drapt back into his doltage," said Farmer Joe-Bob Grissom, who had gone to the major's for the purpose of discussing the matter. "An' yit, they do say that he's got a clean title to every bit of the prop'ty, ef you take into account all that talk about his wife's brother, an' sech like."

"Well," remarked the major grimly, "Sarah there ain't got no brother, an' I reckon I'm sorter pretected from them kind of gwines-on."

"Why, tooby shore you are," said his wife, who was the Sarah referred to; "but I ain't so mighty certain that I wouldn't be better off if I had a brother to follow you around where the wimmen folks can't go. You've flung away many a bright dollar that he might have picked up."

"Who, Sarah?" inquired the major, wincing a little.

"My brother," returned Mrs. Bass.

"Why, you haven't got a brother, Sarah," said Major Bass.

"More's the pity," exclaimed the major's wife. "I ought to have had one, a great big double-j'inted chap. But you needn't tell me about the old Judge," she went on.

"He tried to out-Yankee the Yankees up yonder in Atlanty, an' now he's a-trying to out-Yankee them down here. Lord! You needn't tell me a thing about old Judge Bascom. Show me a man that's been wrapped up with the Radicals, and I'll show you a man that ain't got no better sense than to try to chousel somebody. I'd just as lief see Underwood have the Bascom Place as the old Judge, every bit and grain."

"Well, I hadn't," said the major emphatically.

"No, ner me nuther," said Mr. Joe-Bob Grissom. "Hit may be right, but hit don't look right. Pap used to say he'd never be happy ontel the Bascoms come back inter the'r prop'ty."

"Well, he's dead, ain't he?" inquired Mrs. Bass in a tone that showed she had the best of the argument.

"Yessum," said Mr. Grissom, shifting about in his chair and crossing his legs, as if anxious to dispose of an unpleasant subject, "yessum, pap's done dead." To this statement, after a somewhat embarrassing silence, he added: "Pap took an' died a long time ago."

"Yes," said Mrs. Bass in a gentler tone, "and I'll warrant you that when he died he was n't pestered 'bout whether the Bascoms owned the Place or not. Did he make any complaints?"

"No 'm," replied Mr. Grissom in a reminiscent way, "I can't say that he did. He jest did n't bother about 'em. Hit looked like they jest natchally slipped outer his mind."

"Why, certainly," said Mrs. Bass, with a little shake of her head; "they slipped outer your pa's mind, and now they say the old Judge has slipped out of his own mind."

"Well, we need n't boast of it, Sarah," remarked the major, with a feeble attempt at severity. "Nobody knows the day when some of us may be twisted around. We 've no room to brag."

"No, we ain't," said his wife, bridling up. "I 've trembled for you a many a day when you thought I was thinking about something else, — a many a day."

"Now you know mighty well, Sarah, that no good-natured man like me ain't a-gwine to up an' lose their mind, jest dry so," said the major earnestly. "They 've got to have some mighty big trouble."

"Yes," said Mrs. Bass, grimly, "and they have to have mind too, I reckon. Nobody that never had a horse ever lost one."

The major nodded his head at Joe-Bob Grissom, as much as to say that it was only a very able man who could afford to have such a sprightly wife. The mute suggestion, however, was lost on Grissom, who was accustomed to taking life seriously.

"I hear a mighty heap of talk," he said, "but I ain't never been so mighty certain an' shore that the old Judge is lost his mind. There'd be lots of fun ef it should happen to be that he had the papers all made out in his pocket, an' I've hearn some hints that-a-way."

"Well," said the more practical Mrs. Bass, "he ain't got no papers. The minute I laid eyes on him after he came back here, I says to Mr. Bass there, 'Mr. Bass,' says I, 'the old Judge has gone wrong in his upper story.' Ah, you can't fool me. I know a thing when I see it, more especially if I look at it close. I've seen folks that had to rub the silver off a thrip to tell whether it was passable or not. I might be fooled about the silver in a thrip, but you can't fool me about a grown man."

"Nobody ain't tryin' to fool you, Sarah," said the major, with some show of spirit.

"Well, I reckon not," exclaimed Mrs. Bass, somewhat contemptuously. "I'd like to see anybody try to fool me right here in my own house and right before my face."

"There ain't no tellin'," said Mr. Joe-Bob Grissom, in his matter-of-fact way, ignoring everything that had been said, — "there ain't no tellin' whether the old Judge is got the papers or not. 'T would be hard on Frank Underwood an' his sister, an' they ain't no better folks than them. They don't make no fuss about it, an' they don't hang out no signs, but when you come to a narrer place in the road where you can't go forrerd nor back'ards, an' nuther can you turn 'roun', you may jest count on them Underwoods. They'll git you out ef you can be got out, an' before you can say thanky-do, they'll be away off yonder helpin' some yuther poor creetur."

"Well," said Major Bass, with an air of independence, "I'm at the fust of it. It may be jest as you say, Joe-Bob; but ef so, I've never knowed it."

"Hit's jest like I tell you," said Joe-Bob, emphatically.

"Well, the Lord love us!" exclaimed Mrs. Bass, "I hope it's so, I do from the bottom of my heart. It would be a mighty queer world if it didn't have some tender spots in it, but you needn't be afraid that they'll ever get as thick as the measles. I reckon you must be renting land on the old Bascom Place," she went on, eying Mr. Grissom somewhat sharply.

"Yessum," said Joe-Bob, moving about uneasily in his chair. "Yessum, I do."

Whereupon Mrs. Bass smiled, and her smile was more significant than anything she could have said. It was disconcerting indeed, and it was not long before Mr. Joe-Bob Grissom made some excuse for depriving Major Jimmy and Mrs. Sarah Bass of his company.

As he was passing the Bascom Place on his way home he saw lights in the house and heard voices on the piazza.

"Ef it warn't for that blamed dog," he thought, "I'd go up there an' see what they er talkin' about so mighty peart."

IX.

But Mr. Grissom's curiosity would not have been satisfied. Judge Bascom was sitting in a large rocking-chair, enjoying the pleasant evening air, and the others were sitting near, talking on the most ordinary topics. This situation was one of the doctor's prescriptions, as Miss Sophie said. Those around were to wear a cheerful air, and the Judge was to be humored in the belief that he was once more the proprietor of the Bascom Place. He seemed to respond to this treatment in the most natural way. The old instinct of hospitality rose in him and had its way. He grew garrulous indeed, and sat on the piazza, or walked up and down and talked by the hour. He was full of plans and projects, and some of them were so suggestive that Francis Underwood made a note of them for further consideration. The Judge was the genial host, and while his daughter was full of grief and humiliation at the position in which she was placed, he appeared to draw new life and inspiration from his surroundings. He took a great fancy to Miss Sophie: her observations, which were practical in the extreme, and often unflattering, were highly relished by him. The Judge himself was a good talker, and he gave Miss Sophie an opportunity to vent some of her pet opinions, the most of which were very pronounced.

As for Mildred, in spite of her grief and anxiety, she found her surroundings vastly more pleasant than she had at first imagined they could be. Some instinct or prepossession made her feel at home in the old house, and as she grew more cheerful and more contented she grew more beautiful and more engaging. At least, this was the opinion of Francis Underwood.

"Brother," said Miss Sophie one day when they were together, "you are in love."

"I don't know whether to say yes or no," he replied. "What is it to be in love?"

"How should I know?" exclaimed Miss Sophie, reddening a little. "I see you mooning around, and moping. Something has come over you, and if it is n't love, what is it?"

He held up his hands, white and muscular, and looked at them. Then he took off his hat and tousled his hair in an effort to smooth it with his fingers.

"It is something," he said after a while "but I don't know what. Is love such an everyday affair that it can be called by name as soon as it arrives?"

"Don't be absurd, brother," said Miss Sophie, with a gesture of protest. "You talk as if you were trying to take a census of the affair."

"No," said he; "I am trying to get a special report. I saw Dr. Bynum looking at you over his spectacles yesterday."

Miss Sophie tried to show that this suggestion was an irritating one, but she failed, and then fell to laughing.

"I never knew I was so full of humor before," said Francis Underwood, by way of comment.

"And I never knew you could be so foolish — to me," said Miss Sophie, still laughing. "What is Dr. Bynum to me?"

"Not having his spectacles to look over, how do I know?"

"But," persisted Miss Sophie, "you need no spectacles to look at Mildred. I have seen you looking at her through your fingers."

"And what was she doing?" inquired Underwood, coloring in the most surprising way.

"Oh," said Miss Sophie, "she was pretending not to notice it; but I can sit with my back to you both and tell by the tone of her voice when this and that thing is going on."

"This, then, is courtship," said Underwood.

"Why, brother, how provoking you are!" exclaimed Miss Sophie. "It is nothing of the sort. It is child's play; it is the way the youngsters do at school. I feel as if I never knew you before; you are full of surprises."

"I surprise myself," he said, with something like a sigh, "and that is the trouble; I don't want to be too surprising."

"But in war," said his sister, "the successful general cannot be too full of surprises."

"In war!" he cried. "Why, I was in hopes the war was over."

"I was thinking about the old saying," she explained — "the old saying that all is fair in love and war."

"Well," said Francis Underwood, "it would be hard to say whether you and Dr. Bynum are engaged in war or not. You are both very sly, but I have seen a good deal of skirmishing going on. Will it end in a serious engagement, with casualties on both sides? The doctor is something of a surgeon, and he can attend to his own wounds, but who is going to look after yours?"

"How can you go on so!" cried Miss Sophie, laughing. "Are we to have an epidemic of delusions?"

"Yes, and illusions too," said her brother. "The atmosphere seems to be full of them. Everything is in a tangle."

And yet it was not long after this conversation that Miss Sophie observed her brother and Mildred Bascom sauntering together under the great cedars, and she concluded that he was trying to untangle the tangle.

There were many such walks, and the old Judge, sitting on the piazza in bright weather, would watch the handsome pair, apparently with a contented air. There was something about this busy and practical young man that filled Mildred's imagination. His individuality was prominent enough to be tantalizing. It was of the dominant variety. In him the instinct of control and command, so pleasing to the feminine mind, was thoroughly developed, and he disposed of his affairs with a promptness and decisiveness that left nothing to be desired.

Everything seemed to be arranged in his mind beforehand.

Everything, that is to say, except his relations with Mildred Bascom. There was not the slightest detail of his various enterprises, from the simplest to the most complicated, with which he was not thoroughly familiar, but this young girl, simple and unaffected as she was, puzzled him sorely. She presented to Francis Underwood's mind the old problem that is always new, and that has as many phases as there are stars in the sky. Here, before his eyes, was a combination for which there was no warrant in his experience — the wit and tenderness of Rosalind, blended with the self-sacrificing devotion of Cordelia. Here was a combination — a complication — of a nature to attract the young man's attention. Problem, puzzle, what you will, it was a very attractive one for him, and he lost no favorable opportunity of studying it.

So the pleasant days came and went. If there were any love-passages between the young people, only the stately cedars or the restless poplars were in the secret, and these told it only to the vagrant west winds that crept over the hills when the silence of night fell over all things.

X.

Those were pleasant days and nights at the old Bascom Place, in spite of the malady with which the Judge was afflicted. They were particularly pleasant when he seemed to be brighter and stronger. But one day, when he seemed to be at his best, the beginning of the end came. He was sitting on the piazza, talking with his daughter and with Francis Underwood. Some reference was made to the Place, when the old Judge suddenly rose from his chair, and, shaking his thin white hand at the young man, cried out:

"I tell you it is mine! The Place always has been mine and it always will be mine."

He tottered forward and would have fallen, but Underwood caught him and placed him in his chair. The old man's nerves had lost their tension, his eyes their brightness. He could only murmur indistinctly, "Mine, mine, mine." He seemed suddenly to have shrunk and shriveled away. His head fell to one side, his face was deadly pale, his lips were blue, and his thin hands clutched convulsively at his clothes and at the chair. Mildred was at his side instantly, but he seemed to be beyond the reach of her voice and beyond the limits of her grief, which was distressful to behold. He tried indeed to stroke the beautiful hair that fell loosely over him as his daughter seized him in her despairing arms, but it was in a vague and wandering way.

Judge Bascom's condition was so alarming that Francis Underwood lifted him in his arms and placed him on the nearest bed, where he lay gazing at the ceiling, sometimes smiling and at other times frowning and crying, "Mine, mine, mine!"

He sank slowly but surely. At the last he smiled and whispered "Home," and so passed away.

He was indeed at home. He had come to the end of his long and tiresome journey. He smiled as he lay sleeping, and his rest was pleasant; for there was that in his dead face, white and pinched as it was, that bore witness to the infinite gentleness and mercy of Christ, who is the Lord.

It was an event that touched the hearts of his old neighbors and their children, and they spoke to one another freely and feelingly about the virtues of the old Judge, the beautiful life he had lived, the distinction he had won, and the mark he had made on his generation. Some, who were old enough to remember, told of his charities in the days when prosperity sat at his board; and in discussing these things the people gradually came to realize the fact that Judge Bascom, in spite of his misfortunes, had shed lustre on his State and on the village in which he was born, and that his renown was based on a character so perfect, and on results so just and beneficent, that all could share in it.

His old neighbors, watching by him as he lay smiling in his dreamless sleep, shortened the long hours of the night with pleasant reminiscences of the dead. Those who sat near the door could see, in an adjoining room, Mildred Bascom sitting at Miss Sophie Underwood's feet, her arms around the older woman's waist. It was a brief and fleeting panorama, as indeed life itself is, but the two, brought together by grief and sympathy, often sat thus in the years that followed. For Mildred Bascom became the mistress of the Bascom Place; and although she has changed her name, the old name still clings to Underwood's domain.